THE LUCKY FORMULA

Jamey French,
Love the Last name !
Have a Lucky Life

THE LUCKY FORMULA

HOW TO STACK THE ODDS IN YOUR FAVOR AND CASH IN ON SUCCESS

MARK LACHANCE

ethos
collective

Published by Ethos Collective
P. O. Box 43, Powell, OH 43065
www.EthosCollective.vip

LCCN: 2021915617
ISBN: 978-1-63680-056-1 (paperback)
ISBN: 978-1-63680-057-8 (hardback)
ISBN: 978-1-63680-058-5 (e-book)

Available in paperback, hardback, e-book, and audiobook.

Dedication

To Mom
You always had our backs and were always on our side.
I will remember you forever as happy-go-lucky.
1946–2021

For special bonus content associated with this book,
including videos, downloads, and
The Lucky Formula Assessment, visit:
TheLuckyFormula.com

Contents

Part 1: My Flaws

Part 2: The Formula

Part 3: Your Future

Foreword

You're here because you know something.
What you know you can't explain, but you feel it.
You've felt it your entire life.
—Morpheus, *The Matrix*

The first time I met Mark Lachance, I knew I found an outlier. This became apparent the moment he started talking about luck (which happened within the first five minutes of our conversation). His perspective didn't compute. It was fresh, unlike anything I've ever heard.

In our industry, you're not supposed to acknowledge luck. In fact, admitting its existence pegs you as naïve and someone to run from. It's the type of word victims obsess over—wielding their concept of luck in two different ways:

1. **It's the reason other people keep winning:** "She's so lucky. No wonder she's so successful. She doesn't even have to try; must be nice."

2. **It's the excuse for or reason why they keep losing.**
   "Things never go my way. I'm so unlucky. Life is against me."

But then I listened to Mark's explanation of luck, and I looked at the results in his life. It blew apart my preconceptions. I quickly realized this guy is an enigma.

Here's why.

He's incredibly intentional about living a high-performance life, unapologetically integrating habits and mindsets uncommon to most. But at the same time, he also acknowledges luck and welcomes it into his daily life, leveraging it to work in his favor.

What gives? Everyone else clings to one or the other.

Luck *or* labor.
Random chance *or* rigorous choice.
A self-made success *or* a beneficiary of happenstance.

Either or—not both and.

As I said, it didn't make sense until I took a deeper dive into Mark's mindset. But when he generously shared it with me, I understood the formula—his formula—*The Lucky Formula*©.

You're about to embark on a new way of *thinking* that will equip you for a new way of *living*.

Learn the formula, and you'll be inspired.

Leverage the formula, and you'll be transformed.

That choice is up to you.

Kary Oberbrunner
Wall Street Journal and *USA Today* bestselling author

Note to the Reader

My guess is that, like most people on planet earth, you're incredibly busy. As a result, you might want "just the facts."

I'll honor you by giving you this option. If you simply want the facts, skip my backstory and hop over to Part 2 to learn The Lucky Formula. A quick word of warning though. If you bypass Part 1, you'll save some time, but you'll also skip out on some transformation. Here's why.

In Part 1, I share some secrets—some big secrets. My flaws! I could have blocked these bruises from making it into the book, but I felt that would be inauthentic. Instead, I believe including the pain from my past will give you greater hope for your future. Besides, if I can leverage The Lucky Formula, then rest assured, you can too.

Whether you start with Part 1 or Part 2, I can't wait to hear how you integrate these concepts into your life and business. Get ready.

Luck is much closer than you think.

—Mark Lachance

Acknowledgments

One condition of The Lucky Formula is to express gratitude, so it's only right that I thank the individuals who have impacted my life. My father and late mother, Guy and Lisa Lachance, influenced my early years. My brothers Scott and Bob, their wives Jacqueline and Beth, and my nieces and nephews Jake, Shane, Ryan, Bobby, Ellie, and Aiden, provided their support. And most importantly, I thank my incredibly supportive family, my wife, Sonya, and sons Lucas and Dylan who continue to inspire me to live lucky.

Special thanks to Max Lehktman and Jack Antaki and the rest of the *awesome* Maxy Media team. I'm thankful for Mark Levy, David Shteif, Stephan Gratziani, Mike Zaidan, Todd Whiton, Denis Platis, William Agoston, Jared Cator, Quentin Rivoire, Jason Nemes, Keith Wilson, JF Durocher, Alex Park, Kevin Lavigne, Nesstor Lopez, Timothy Canivel, Cynthia Ibrahim, Rome Mufalo, Ariane P. Goyette, Reggie Gaby, Christelle Fethiere, Mark Addy, Andreas Johansson, Jaroslav Spacek, Anders Myrvold, Terry Virtue, Kevin Lambrix, Nick Tritton, Renan Puglia, Fabio Holanda, Philip

Fayer, Rod Leblanc, Lester Fernandes, Jeff Google, Michel Fillion, Benoit Gosselin, Mo Abdulai, Marc Cormier, Tony Romano, Denise Doherty, Craig MacDonald, Mous Kamal el Dine, Dr. Daniel Crisafi, Dr. Srini Pillay, Kim White, Steve Fryer, Dan Sullivan, and Tony Robbins and all of my YouTube and podcast mentors for their advice, coaching, support, and encouragement.

Finally, to Kary Oberbrunner, Lori Piotrowski, and Denae Hively—thank you for bringing *The Lucky Formula* to life.

Introduction

Ability is of little value without opportunity.
I had rather my generals be lucky than able.
—Napoleon Bonaparte

The year was 2007.

Fear gripped the world at the height of the Great Recession. I racked my brain. What the hell happened?

Bills piled up on my desk. Where did they come from? Most of them didn't even register. All I knew was I owed money to more people and places than I could count. I was on the verge of bankruptcy and utter failure.

There wasn't going to be anything left for me at the end— if I even survived. The cash in my bank account drained lower and lower. My thoughts raced. How would I get out of this hole? Anxiety ripped into my heart, tearing away any remaining scraps of confidence.

A few years prior, I was riding high. Flush with fresh cash, I embodied hope and optimism. A young millionaire, I helped lead a Canadian company, taking them from zero to an industry-leading success story.

On the back of that success, I was hungry for my next big win. This time I craved global domination. I had my sights on becoming a billionaire. But then that lofty dream—and the money that supported it—came crashing down. I made a mistake or series of mistakes. My downfall became my reality. In hindsight, I shouldn't have made such mistakes, but I didn't know better at the time.

Chalk it up to naivete or arrogance. I was too ambitious.

How did I get here? I mean, how did I truly get here?

I knew the answer. Who was I kidding? I convinced myself I'd be successful come hell or high water, and I fought as hard as I could. I willed my way into success. But I soon learned that effort alone doesn't pay the bills.

I willed my way into success. But I soon learned that effort alone doesn't pay the bills.

Comparing these two people, who I am now and who I was then, there's a complete disconnect between the two. If I were an outsider, I'd think, "Hell no, these two people can't be the same damn person!"

My personality, the way I do business, how I treat my own health, and the things I prioritize were all so different back then. I nearly ruined myself.

Thankfully, today that's all changed. Be encouraged. No matter how much you think you're stuck, change is possible. My story proves this. All those "rules" getting in your way might not be rules at all. Maybe they're just fabricated self-limiting beliefs holding you back from your ideal future.

Are you done waiting for chance to smile upon you?

Are you ready to start stacking the odds in your favor and cash in on success in work and life?

If so, keep reading.

✿ ✿ ✿

I eventually clawed my way out of the darkness and into the light. I extracted these valuable lessons from those times of struggle. Then I put them to the test in the real world. To my surprise, life started going my way. I began to get lucky.

Other people noticed and asked me for my "secret." I shared The Lucky Formula with them, and they began enjoying the results too. Fast-forward life, and I've heard this same testimony from countless others. They've leveraged the formula and reaped the benefits for themselves and their loved ones.

So how does someone leverage luck in their daily life?

I've asked myself this question many times. After all, I've always considered myself to be a lucky person. Whenever I thought I hit my "rock bottom," an opportunity to level up presented itself. Other times, I started initiatives that simply took off without any resistance.

I consider my life blessed. Many lucky breaks came my way, especially when I needed them. But as I reflected and studied what I achieved and accomplished, all the times I hit lows and then highs, I noticed these were not just lucky events. At each juncture, I discovered how a few clear choices and specific actions shaped what I originally labeled as a "lucky outcome."

Luck is a force—and you can harness its power if you learn the formula and leverage the formula. Unfortunately, many people perceive luck as something uncontrollable or random, like the weather that simply comes upon us. This is ignorant.

Luck is a force—and you can harness its power if you learn the formula and leverage the formula.

Sure, I've had moments when I felt lucky and other moments when I felt unlucky. But I made the lucky moments matter by making the most out of them. Conversely, I never allowed my unlucky moments to undo me.

Are you currently stuck in the "gutter" of life? Are you dissatisfied with your job, relationships, or health? Maybe you've always dreamed of a successful life but never dared to go after it. Or perhaps you're already doing great, but you know you have more in you.

Regardless of what brought us together, I'm sincerely glad you decided to pick up this book. If you're flying high at the moment, you'll benefit from *The Lucky Formula* because it will help you create sustainable success, not just random good fortune. If you're experiencing deep lows or despairing woes, you'll learn how to make life work for you, not against you.

I know from firsthand experience life can feel cruel. But believe me when I tell you your luck can change in a moment. The way you view luck is directly tied to the way you view life. Most people see themselves as a passenger simply along for the ride. In this book, I'll invite you back into the driver's seat and point you in the direction of your ideal future.

The journey we're about to take isn't an easy one. It's going to take some serious focus. The Lucky Formula only works for those willing to work. But those who do will soon create the life of their dreams.

PART 1

My Flaws

1

Origin Story

Nothing in this world can take the place of persistence.
Talent will not; nothing is more common than
unsuccessful men with talent. Genius will not;
unrewarded genius is almost a proverb.
Education will not; the world is full of educated derelicts.
Persistence and determination alone are omnipotent.
—Calvin Coolidge

On most summer days as a teenager, I bolted out of bed at 5:30 a.m., thanks to the unforgiving alarm clock. Peering out the window, I confronted the fate awaiting me. The orange sun creeping over the treetops foreshadowed my future. I'd soon be grinding away on a scorching hot, black tar roof. On those blazing days, the sun bore down on us, mimicking a big panini press.

Back then, I worked with my dad's construction crew to earn money for college. The grueling work seemed unbearable.

Nowadays, sitting in my comfortable office, I reflect on those thoughts whenever I'm tempted to feel tired. That quick trip down memory lane jerks me back to a place of gratitude.

If you asked that kid, toiling away on the roof, if someday he would be a millionaire running a media business, his mind would explode. Today I am healthy. I have a beautiful family. And I am leading a highly successful business I love.

I have been many things in my career: a sports agent who made big deals in the National Hockey League, a CEO of a large payments' company, an owner of a well-known recording studio, and a founder of a fitness company.

Currently, I am the CEO of a performance marketing agency. I have held shares of companies that went from zero to public four times in my life, ridden the highs of the dot-com bubble, and crashed with the lows of the Great Recession. I have earned millions of dollars. I have lost millions of dollars.

Despite all of this, I always go back to the time I spent with my dad. He was the first person who taught me the basics, like hard work, integrity, and self-improvement. These became my first lessons in luck.

In the following years, I learned how to leverage luck. Opportunities awaited me at every corner. I wasted many of them away, but I learned how to make the most of these opportunities at some point. I learned being lucky is not a result of random chance but rather something that can be controlled and even crafted.

I learned being lucky is not a result of random chance but rather something that can be controlled and even crafted.

Steve Jobs shared an interesting perspective: "You can't connect the dots looking forward; you can only connect them looking backward. So you have to trust that the dots will somehow connect in your future."

He's right. In hindsight, we can attribute everything to anything. We can talk about how a soccer player showed early excellence when he played for the high school team. At the same time, we'll ignore that he only turned to soccer after an injury that made him switch from his true passion, football.

The truth is, we have no idea how our lives are going to turn out. Steve Jobs was right. Guessing where the dots will be—that's the real hard part.

I believe your environment matters to a degree, and you often don't have any control over how, where, and to whom you are born. You can have the best genes for mathematics, but if you come from a household that pays zero attention to your education, your talent will most likely go nowhere.

My upbringing mattered. I was born in Lewiston, Maine, on December 13, 1969. I came from a rural family background, rooted in Eastern Quebec. My ancestors were hard-working farmers, tilling the land, taking in the harvest, ensuring all their children worked in the fields.

My grandfather started as a farmer and then made a living as a lumberjack providing for his wife and kids. Then, they moved to the ghetto, and I don't know how he managed eight kids while only speaking French, but he did. The most incredible part was that every single one of those kids moved out of the ghetto. They didn't take any handouts from anyone, and nobody gave them anything. They did it the old-fashioned way, with hard work.

My dad was one of them, and by the time he had me, he'd adopted a strong work ethic. Needless to say, I grew up in a household that valued what we now call hustle.

My father served in the military, and fortunately, despite all his years in the army, he missed the window on being deployed to the Vietnam War. After his military service, he worked in construction, and we frequently moved—from Maine to Virginia to Massachusetts and finally to Connecticut.

My father started his own company when I was nine or ten years old. Although he initially worked with his brother, they parted ways shortly after. Autonomy mattered to my father, and he didn't like other people telling him what he could or could not do.

Even as a young child, I could see that running a construction company was difficult work. My father woke up early in the morning, before anyone else, and left at 6:00 a.m. He would return around 6:00 p.m., and after a brief dinner, he'd keep working, doing estimates and drawing up plans until 10:00 or 11:00 p.m. almost every single night.

It seems as though he wanted to pass this mindset onto me. When I was fourteen or fifteen, my father decided it was time for me to start working. The remnants of the Oil Shock Crisis of 1979 still lingered, and in the early eighties, a recession swept through the economy.

My father sat me down and told me he wanted to put me through college, but he did not have enough money because of the recession. The only way I could make up the difference was if I worked in the summers. So each summer from 1984 until 1992, I joined his construction crew. I sweated and toiled on the roof during those 102-degree scorching days.

Those summer days taught me a valuable lesson. I learned the true value of a full day's work, and I gained a genuine respect for work and earning my keep. I also realized I didn't want to do this for the rest of my life. I committed never to slack off because the construction business sucked big time.

I grew up in a family that deeply cared about ice hockey, and every weekend we played games at the arena. My parents sometimes drove my two brothers and me up to four games each on the weekend. This meant up to twelve games on Saturdays and Sundays. It was crazy, but that was what every hockey family did. Hockey was all about putting effort and work into it, and that included the parents.

In hockey, like any other sport, many athletes go far on pure talent. But then they always hit a wall. There's a ceiling they can't break through unless they put in a ton of extra work.

My brother Scott was tough, and he could tear it up on the ice, but his work ethic was unbelievable. One summer, I witnessed this when I came home from college. I lived in a frat house during the semester, living the typical frat boy life—partying regularly. Scott was in the backyard, doing push-ups and sit-ups and firing pucks in the backyard rink. He fired a thousand pucks a day. Scott modeled what it took to be a pro, and it reminded me that in all things I do, I would have to work as hard as I could to be successful.

I took it to heart. When I worked on my father's construction projects during those summers, I aimed to be the best guy on the crew. I wanted to work hard, but I also wanted to do the best work possible.

❉ ❉ ❉

My father valued personal development, evidenced by his passion for Dale Carnegie classes. When I was ten years old, he sat down my two brothers and me and had us write our goals for the next ten, twenty, and thirty years. At the time, I wasn't exactly sure what was going on, but that was the point. He wanted to instill habits inside us. I remember us writing out something like "go to college on a full scholarship, play in the Olympics, play in the National Hockey League, and be successful."

For Scott, it would come true—all of it. Scott received a full ride to Boston University, played on the US Olympics Team in France in 1992, then went on to play for the New York Islanders, Montreal Canadiens, Vancouver Canucks, and Columbus Blue Jackets for many years. He enjoyed an illustrious sports career before retiring in his thirties. Heck, the guy has his own Wikipedia page. He achieved all of his goals.

My other brother Bob achieved most of his goals. He received a full ride to Boston University as well. The St. Louis Blues drafted him, and he also went on to enjoy a hockey career that spanned over a decade.

That left me, the runt of the litter. Scott is six-foot-two. Bob is six feet tall. I'm by far the smallest of the three, and I didn't come close to playing in the National Hockey League.

This was beside the point. My father's insistence upon us writing our goals down when I was ten wasn't about me knowing exactly where I wanted to go. Instead, he wanted us to have a direction—an objective to move toward. Drifting aimlessly wasn't part of my dad's plan for us, although many other kids in the neighborhood chose that future.

My dad encouraged us to read books that would instill in us the value of personal development. The first book he gave us was *Think and Grow Rich* by Napoleon Hill. Next, he gave us *Awaken the Giant Within* by Tony Robbins.

I soaked up all the lessons I heard. In *Think and Grow Rich*, I read about visualization. This is the process of imagining a place you want to be or achieving what you want to achieve. It's putting your faith in what you visualize, then making it happen.

One day I woke up and thought to myself, *You know what, I'm going to score three goals in my next game—no matter what happens.* And then I pictured that in my mind a thousand times the night before the game happened. Not only that, but I visualized exactly how I would score those three goals. One would be from the point; I would rip a slapshot right over the goaltender's shoulder. SCORE! The next one, I would put the puck through the goaltender's legs. SCORE! And on the next one, I would put the puck low stick side. SCORE!

In my mind, I saw myself doing it over and over again, and lo and behold, I scored three goals that game. It was a moment of realization for me, not only that visualization actually works, but why personal development has so much to offer. That made a big impression on me as a kid, and it has continued throughout my adult life.

I started to realize that education transcends what you learn at school. Reading these books taught me there was so much more to knowledge than passively taking in information and memorizing phrases. Learning how to learn was even more useful than learning a strong work ethic. This was one of the greatest lessons my father taught me.

Education transcends what you learn at school.

❦ ❦ ❦

In high school, I lost interest in classroom lectures and fell behind. The topics and the teachers disengaged me. I can't remember any of them sparking my interest.

Finishing high school well enough to get to university was the only thing that mattered to me, and I achieved that goal. I went to Bentley University, known for its accounting and finance programs.

It was not an easy choice because school cost a large amount of money. At the time, tuition was around $15,000 a year, which was a hefty sum for my family, even after all that work I put in during the summer to save cash. But I went for it because I thought finance was what you had to study to make money. I didn't just want to make money; I wanted to make a ton of money. Like many others, I wanted to have a big house, a beautiful car, and the finer things in life. Because I had no clue how to do that, studying finance seemed like the smartest option for me.

Despite my lack of studying, I had a great time at university. We jokingly called my study method the BAC-BAC-D method. I learned it from a friend. On multiple-choice tests, I marked B, A, C, B, A, C, D, then repeated that until the end. School simply didn't interest me much.

Although my GPA was a 2.8, I excelled at throwing parties. I joined a fraternity on campus and earned the role of chairing the party committee. Hardly an academic, I embodied a hustler instead. During sophomore year, I needed to get some cash, so I started working for a valet company in downtown Boston. I pulled in $500 to $600 a night—not bad for a college student.

Though my time in college was a blur of parties, money-making efforts, and mediocre grades, it proved significant. Some might say I wasted my years along with my fees, but I don't consider it that way. On the contrary, college remains one of my favorite times in my life. And frankly, I still use the accounting and finance skills I learned back in school.

The most important thing I took away from my college days was what I learned about myself and the people around me. That experience taught me how to interact with others and get out of my comfort zone. Although I stayed in my shell in high school, I bloomed into a more diverse human being in university.

❀ ❀ ❀

Eventually, I had to decide on what to do after graduating. Back then, Microsoft earned the reputation as the hot shot tech company, and it took off like a rocket ship. Their representatives came to campus several times for recruitment. After that, I thought I might leave for Seattle to become a programmer.

Many of my classmates took another route: Wall Street. One friend worked as a trader for Citibank® and got me an interview there. I had many options available to me, but I didn't know which one to take. They all felt like excellent opportunities.

Then, because of my brother Scott's success, I met some sports agents. Scott was a highly sought-after talent, so naturally, I met the agents who tried to recruit him. From what they said, it sounded like a life out of the movies—*Jerry Maguire*, in fact. They frequented the hockey rink, recruiting athletes and negotiating contracts. They flew all over the world. They made great money. I said to myself, "This is the life I want." I craved becoming a sports agent. Unfortunately, I knew it meant starting from zero.

Because of this, I returned to my father's construction crew since it was a reliable gig. Moreover, at $40,000 a year, it paid better than many other jobs available for recent graduates. And so, in 1992, with a struggling global economy, I moved back home to work with my father. It turned out to be one of the best decisions I could make.

On the weekdays, I worked on my father's construction crew. And on the weekends, I worked for a sports agent. I would find him players, and he would represent them. I was the guy in the rinks, watching the players and talking to the parents. This was the only part I didn't like. I hated talking to the parents because they gave me a crooked eye, worried I would somehow steer their sons in the wrong direction.

I loved traveling and watching talented hockey players. There's something about observing high performers getting it done the right way, that gets me going. After the games, I'd hang out with these amazing athletes and bang out a negotiation.

The day finally came when I realized I was done working for my father. Ironically, my father recognized this at the same time. I walked into his office to announce my resignation, and he told me he had planned to fire me anyway. He didn't want me to be attached to his business any longer. He wanted me to get out there to do bigger things because he saw that fiery passion inside me.

I took a job at a plastics company in Boston. I became the sales rep in the eastern region, New England, to be specific, all the while keeping up my sports agent career. This region was ranked dead last in the country. I took it to the second-place region within six months quite easily. Looking back, I realize sales came easy to me.

My success in sales was tied to how much effort I put into it, so the work ethic I'd learned from my father all those years ago made success come easy. I showed up, made the calls, then asked for the sale. That's it. I did the actual work of selling day in and day out, and it all came together.

Despite my obvious success, I hated every moment of it. The entire process felt tedious and relentless. I needed something different—something that challenged me. After all, who could really get excited about selling plastic forks? At that moment, I knew I was built for something more.

Despite my obvious success, I hated every moment of it.

To top that all off, the boss was, to put it simply and elegantly, an asshole. This experience confirmed my desire to build a more independent career, one where I had control. Though he was a pretty cool guy after hours, my boss loved to grind me down during work.

All of this led to a growing sense of discontent. That was the last job I worked for somebody else or for something I didn't have a stake in.

Through the hockey recruitment experience with Scott, I connected with Steve Fryer, who is now a legend in the sports industry. After Steve mentored me to the amazing life of being a sports agent, I started by representing my youngest brother, Bob. He was drafted by the St. Louis Blues and played for the Worcester IceCats, the minor league feeder team of the St. Louis Blues.

During one particular game, a player named Andreas Johansson caught my attention. The player I had just watched artfully weave on the ice impressed me. I asked my brother to introduce us.

I immediately started building rapport, taking him out to dinners and asking about his relationship with his current agent. Whoever his agent was, I was going to get him because, as far as I saw it, his talent and skill were being wasted. So every chance I got, I'd pepper Johansson with requests to represent him.

He didn't budge, but I persisted. I was determined to get this guy. Then, around Thanksgiving, I got his call. At the time, the coach of the Worcester IceCats had a prejudice against European players. It was pretty widespread amongst coaches at the time. They thought Europeans were soft, and they looked down upon them because many wouldn't fight anyone.

As you might know, in North America, it's a tradition to put on a show for the fans, dropping the gloves and throwing punches. But in Europe, this type of behavior can result in a multi-game suspension. There's a huge cultural difference.

Of course, the coach wasn't aware of this nuance, and, as a result, Johansson got less time on the ice—all because he wouldn't drop his gloves and get into a fistfight. Johansson was flabbergasted because he assumed they were paying him to play hockey, not get into fights with other players. Johansson was a leading scorer in the Swedish hockey league, and over here, he got benched because he didn't try to smash someone's face. One day, he dropped the gloves against a tough guy on the other team, and, in turn, he got his face beaten to a pulp. Johansson was sent right to the hospital, where they had to put pins and plates in his face.

Five days later, after not hearing from his agent, he called me and asked me to represent him.

Immediately I went to work on getting Johansson's career going. He was a great player, and anybody with an eye for hockey could see that. I had a good relationship with the New York Islanders' general manager, and I was able to get Johansson out of Worcester. I moved him from the American Hockey League to Salt Lake City in the International Hockey League, also an affiliate of the New York Islanders. That was huge for him because Johansson flourished under coach Butch Goring, who respected talent for what it was. Johansson thanked me big time. Ultimately, that was his catalyst for playing in the National Hockey League.

Subsequently, Johansson opened the door for me to a goldmine of players from Europe, particularly Sweden. Around this time, a European wave began to hit the game. Through Johansson, I connected with players I ultimately represented in the NHL, like Fredrik Olausson, Peter Nordstrom, Anders Myrvold, and Jaroslav Spacek, among many others. I'd fly to Sweden every summer with Johansson and stay with him for a week. These times in Sweden were possibly the best times of my agent days.

❀ ❀ ❀

Over time, I became disillusioned with the agent business. I knew no matter how much effort I put into it, I could still lose everything. Even if my clients were satisfied, even if I got them the best deals possible for their future, they could still turn around and drop me for no reason.

When working with another player from the New York Islanders, I secured him a good contract with great money. Then he fired me, and he signed with the Ottawa Senators for less money in the following year. I was so confused because there was no reason to do this. I had done a great job and was fired, nonetheless. I never got a straight answer for it.

The agent business was also far too cutthroat for the amount of work I did. Just as I had poached my clients from other agents, I was easily robbed of my clients by somebody singing a better song than me.

Years later, that was how Johansson slipped away from me—or, rather, how another agent took him from me. He was my friend, the guy I had given his first big break in the NHL. I was in Boston at the time, and he was in New York, so it was hard to reach him and easy for anyone close to him to poach him away. I knew exactly what had happened. Somebody else whispered promises to Johansson, and he switched agents. Ironically, that was exactly how I got Johansson in the first place, by being there while the other agent wasn't.

That situation changed my perspective on the agent business. I realized there was no point to any of the efforts I had built up when it could all be yanked away at any moment, for any reason—or no reason at all. None of the good relationships I had established with any player mattered because when you have to be cutthroat to find any success, it becomes difficult to trust the people you work with. When you combine that with how arbitrary these business decisions tended to be, I realized my work ethic was useless as a sports agent.

I knew there was another thing out there that could give me something better. I was done hustling for minimal gains. I responded by answering the call to adventure and quitting the business altogether.

Little did I know back then, this simple choice moved me closer to discovering The Lucky Formula.

2

Call to Adventure

The purpose of life, after all, is to live it, to taste
experience to the utmost, to reach out eagerly and
without fear for a newer and richer experience.
—Eleanor Roosevelt

Toward the end of my career as a sports agent, I ran
into someone who introduced me to another line of
business. This guy had a payment processing company, and he was about my age, twenty-seven years old. He
drove a Porsche and made $15,000 to $20,000 a month. Even
today, that's a fair amount of money to make in one month.
I had to know more about what he was doing. Upon further inquiry, he mentioned he was making recurring revenue
from his company. He had around 2000 clients, and he was
laughing all the way to the bank every month. So I thought
to myself, "That's a hell of a business. He literally could stop
working right now if he wanted to."

When I compared his earnings to mine, what I was doing seemed absolutely ridiculous. I was working from client to client, pouring countless hours into each one. Basically, my hours of effort were the only things moving the business forward. Ingrained in me from what I had learned working with my father, this habit of overworking myself for little benefit was beginning to get old.

I pushed myself with sheer force of will, driving my career forward with hustle and effort. Ultimately, when considering the Porsche guy, I knew working by the hour wasn't something I was interested in at all.

With my hustle, I knew I could take it to an even greater level. As a result, I started my own payments' company, ProNet International, with my girlfriend at the time. It was essentially a two-person company. I brought in the sales and did the marketing and she focused on the operations.

We started by using my strategy of going after international dot-coms that couldn't process credit card transactions themselves. In the late nineties, banks weren't giving merchant accounts, and it was very difficult to get credit card processing capacity on websites.

I saw a massive opportunity, so the first part of my strategy was setting up meetings with all the internet

The Lucky Formula was beginning to emerge, and I was experiencing the benefits.

service providers in Montreal and Ottawa. I also contacted the US consulate, and they set up twenty-five meetings for me over the course of five days. I received many contracts and referrals from merchants who needed to process credit cards online. The volume of business was incredible. Many people told me I was lucky to hit the jackpot like this. I knew differently. The Lucky Formula was beginning to emerge, and I was experiencing the benefits.

I met a certain CEO of a company at this time—I'll call him Joe. He saw what I was doing and recognized the potential of it. This was when the dot-com boom was going absolutely crazy. He understood that we could process transactions online for merchants, and he noticed how he could take advantage of what we had to offer. Joe wanted to build something big, a brand for the new digital age, and slap a dot-com onto it. He would combine a web development company, an IT company, and a digital advertising agency to make a bigger company that would launch in the public markets.

Like some kind of Transformer© robot coming together, Joe would combine it all into a super robot. He spun an elaborate and grandiose story about how we would become the biggest web service provider in the world. The investors swooned at the narrative, and the stock debuted with big fanfare. The share price eventually skyrocketed. My shares started at something like $0.25, and they shot up to around $10.50. I became one of those paper millionaires in the news.

I felt nothing but pure ecstasy. I thought I had entered the big leagues now. This was where my financial status was going to take off. I was worth around close to three million dollars, and for a guy in his late twenties, I thought I was on top of the world. Unfortunately, I was drunk on that feeling, and it led to my downfall.

In hindsight, Joe's plan was a house of cards. At the time, I believed in him. I genuinely thought he would build this mega-company, but as the years went by, I realized he wasn't going to build anything. He got people to believe him because he told a great story, but he never provided any substance.

Then the market crashed. In the end, all I received from this amazing ride was a $40,000-dollar tax bill. It felt like I got the wind knocked out of me. Staring at this enormous tax bill, I was numb, unable to say or do anything. I knew it was over—at least for now.

My story didn't end there. In the process, I became good friends with the CEO of another payments' company. That guy knew of my ability to motivate and hire a sales team. He had a grand plan to build a massive company and dominate the payments' industry. As a part of this strategy, he needed a vice president of sales, and he thought I would be a perfect fit.

"Why don't you come to Montreal?" he asked. "I'll give you 10 percent equity in the company." I was sold on the spot. Plus, I had been in love with Montreal since a young age, and I had always seen myself living there. It checked all the boxes. He offered me a position, and I moved to Canada in my early thirties.

Confession: One of the things I struggle with to this day is when I'm leaving one thing for another. I can't decide if I'm leaving it because I'm giving up. On the one hand, I don't want to admit defeat or leave something unfinished. But I also don't want to miss out on a better opportunity.

In the case of leaving Boston for Montreal, I believe I made the right move. My time with ProNet and the public company that bought it was essentially finished, and I needed a fresh start.

I came into the new company, Pivotal Payments, when it was just getting started. I brought ample industry experience, and I was the number three hire.

The founder was a brilliant man. He stumbled upon this opportunity in the payments' domain, and he dropped out of university to jump headfirst into it. In a way, his story was the classic tech entrepreneur tale.

He was young, and, as far as I could tell, he was a genius. But as all young geniuses go, his attitude and approach were raw. Thus, I felt it was my job to rein him in and coach him to be someone people could lean on. He tended to be hard-charging, which was great when maneuvering in the cutthroat payment space. When dealing with internal staff, however, he needed to tone down these tendencies.

I was one of the few people capable of standing up to him. Since no one else dared to confront the company's founder, I tried to soften him and keep him on the same page as everyone else. This man's brain worked at an exhilarating pace, and I needed to keep my debating skills sharp. I had to be ready at a moment's notice to lock horns with him if necessary. It felt chaotic at times, but I liked the man. From his relentless approach, I learned a ton about managing a large organization.

My job was to get more sales for the company, and that is exactly what I accomplished. I brought in every single sale until I started hiring a sales team to scale up our revenue. For six years, I ran myself ragged. It was a ton of work—getting sales, hiring people, and motivating them to do their best.

Nonetheless, I enjoyed it.

I had a great sales team, and most of all, I loved helping them achieve a huge level of success. For me, when I teach somebody something and they're successful, it feels great. That is what I strive for. I love to coach and help others. If a salesperson on my team brought a potential sale into my office, we would both get on the phone and nail it. Then once we succeeded, it got me going even more. It was a positive feedback cycle of motivation.

This was a huge moment of self-discovery. Until Pivotal, I mostly flew solo in all my past careers after college. My time with Pivotal was the first time I had grown a large company from the ground up, and it taught me how rewarding it could be to ensure the success of others. It boosted my morale and motivated me to continue investing in people, positively affecting the entire company.

During my days at Pivotal, I went from being the third person hired to building a strong sales team and an entire staff of 240 people. We went from zero revenue to multi-millions per month in processing volume by the time I left. I never knew until then I had what it took to build a company like that, so it was a huge confidence builder. It enabled me to think bigger and beat the odds.

Pivotal was also where I developed a sense for managing people. I quickly caught on to the best way to approach certain people. I gravitated toward a style in which I managed my employees to empower them in a positive manner. In order to get there, however, sometimes I also had to rip into people.

Other times, I had to be extremely blunt. Certain employees just wanted to be praised, and that was more than enough to keep them going. I had to understand what kind of person I was dealing with before anything else. Everybody needs to be managed in a different way that suits their particular needs.

I also learned how to command a room. When I walked into a boardroom full of powerful money people who, on paper, exerted control over me,

Everybody needs to be managed in a different way that suits their particular needs.

I would storm in there like I owned the room. People indeed feel your power as much as you exude it, and that makes everything easier. Of course, I went up against the fighters and bullies, but that was all the more reason to display confidence because I knew I deserved to be there.

At the end of the day, though, it was time to run my own ship because I stopped growing.

To prepare for a smooth exit, I sold my shares in the company for millions of dollars. I could now do whatever I wanted to do and succeed. After all, I had the know-how. I was ready for it. With the money in hand and experience gained, I was ready to build my own company. The Lucky Formula was taking shape.

3

Dark Days

We are all failures—at least, the best of us are.
—J.M. Barrie

When I left Pivotal, I acquired a bunch of capital from selling my shares. Thrilled for my fresh start, I emerged with a chance to build something under my control. With my connections, experience, and cash, I convinced myself I would make something big happen.

Around this time, I received a call from the CFO of a company in Montreal saying he was looking for someone to help build their corporation. This firm offered me the positions of president and Co-CEO, as well as some equity. I'm not sure how much it was, but it was enough to catch my interest.

Though it was a big opportunity, it wasn't what I had really wanted. I was looking for partners to work with, not to join another company already existing. Still, I thought it could be a great chance to put zero dollars in, get equity in a company, and run it as president and Co-CEO. I liked the idea of being in control and doing what I needed to do to build a sales team. They told me I would have a hefty budget at my disposal for growing the team, and after negotiating a favorable deal, I joined the company.

On my first day, I walked in fired up. I couldn't wait to build something amazing—and have a nice story to talk about someday. I was motivated to crush the competition—in my mind, Pivotal.

I laughed at the thought.

Right off the bat, the guy who hired me told me we couldn't get a sales team yet because we didn't have the budget. That was the beginning of many broken promises.

In my first week, I went on a business trip to Vancouver to visit the head office. I met the board and some of the investors. At that meeting, I learned we didn't have the capital the firm had promised. When it came to my salary, they only agreed to pay me half of what we had originally agreed upon. I thought to myself, *Are they kidding?* I was getting paid a fortune back in Pivotal compared to this.

I had to scrap everything I had imagined in the beginning. I had planned on hiring a sales team of twenty-five people, but they had no cash for it. They were, in fact, still in the process of raising money. Thus, whatever business plan I drew up was tossed aside. Understandably it didn't take long, probably a week or so, before the job lost its appeal.

I told the founders I was leaving because I didn't appreciate that they were dishonest with me from the beginning.

In the end, I told the founders I was leaving because I didn't appreciate the fact that they were dishonest with me from the beginning. My superpower was hiring, training, and motivating a sales team, which was one of the main reasons I'd come over to this company.

They didn't take this too well because we had already negotiated for an equity deal. In fact, I was threatened with a lawsuit to get me to spit those shares back. But one of the board members said I deserved those shares and saw the situation for what it was. Besides, they were crunched for money anyway. They didn't have the capacity for legal fees. And even if they did sue me, I would've stood my ground because I knew my value. I had built a highly profitable company consisting of hundreds of amazing employees. I knew how to do my job and how to sell in both the US and Canadian marketplaces since I had the confidence and the know-how to do it.

That ended my short stint at this company. A few years after the company went public, I received a bit of a windfall, but more important than that, I listened to my gut.

☘ ☘ ☘

When I stepped away from that company, I looked elsewhere to launch my own company. I was determined to create a brilliant business. I first had to raise money to build a team of my own. I set up meetings up and down the East Coast, from Montreal to Florida, to find investors open to my idea.

In my search for investors, I came across a so-called real estate guru in Wellington, Florida, through my wife's introduction. He had twenty-five acres of land, thirty horses, and a gigantic mansion. Strangely, he had no furniture in his house. I thought it odd, but I shrugged it off. He liked my story and was willing to invest in me. As we continued to talk, he told me he had another rich friend who had a chain of gas stations in Florida, and I thought I had hit my goldmine. I pitched my business idea to him, and he liked it. He seemed enthusiastic, and I thought I had found a good potential partner.

Unfortunately, the guru never called me back. Weeks passed, and I thought, *Maybe he just got cold feet.* So I began looking around for another partner. Several months later, I finally got a call from the guru. He told me he was in Montreal. He wanted me to come visit him at this hotel just outside the city. This guy was supposed to be filthy rich, but he was staying at a cheap hotel. Nevertheless, I was energized by his phone call because I was eager to get business started.

When I arrived, he had all these plans laid out, and instead of talking about my idea, he pitched me on a real estate deal. He told me about this opportunity north of Montreal. In 2006, the real estate market was as hot as it could be, and the Brits were rolling into town and buying up real estate all over the place because of the stupidly cheap currency. In a place called Morin-Heights, he was planning a resort development project. He talked about similar projects at Fiddler Lake and Blueberry Lake, resort properties that had sold out within weeks of launching their London deals.

This definitely perked up my ears because it sounded like a sure deal. I knew about the real estate market's craze, and this golden opportunity seemed set in stone. Even though it wasn't the business I had originally planned to go into, it felt like the perfect opportunity. I still had money from selling my Pivotal shares, so I had the resources to move forward.

But there was something different about this development project. The guru planned to build it in Morin-Heights around the famous recording studio called Le Studio, one of the most influential recording studios in modern music history.

About an hour from Montreal, Morin-Heights is mainly a tourist town, like so many villages within that distance from the city. People come from all over for skiing, hiking, mountain biking, and other outdoor recreational activities. Adorned with a small but adorable downtown area, city people craving a breath of fresh air frequent this picturesque space.

Surprisingly, this village is rich with modern music history. World-famous artists—Sting, Rush, Bee Gees, Chicago, The Rolling Stones, Celine Dion, and David Bowie, among many others—recorded their music here.

People look around and think, *Really? Here? In the middle of nowhere?* But it's true. This is exactly what happened. Le Studio was built by Andre Perry, a recording engineer who worked for John Lennon. He owned a lake in Morin-Heights and built a large high-tech studio equipped with accommodation for the artists.

This studio was such a big deal that in 1986 it issued its stock on the Montreal Stock Exchange, netting almost $4 million as a result. Then Perry sold the studio in 1988. It changed hands multiple times, once owned by the company known for organizing the Montreal International Jazz Festival until it fell to disrepair and disuse in the 2000s.

Back in the eighties, when Le Studio's fame was at its height, this place was an institution—a rock no one could dislodge from the place it managed to carve out. Popular bands came from all over to record their entire albums here at this musical fortress. The first day I pulled up in my vehicle to Le Studio, the groundskeeper greeted me and told me his name was Richard. I smiled, realizing I was in the presence of a person who never left the seventies. His hair reached down to his band memorabilia, pinned proudly to his big winter jacket. In between his chain-smoking, he spoke at a ferocious pace.

He told me his thoughts on what we could do with the land, the possibility of rebuilding an even bigger and better studio. Yet I sensed his sadness and state of mourning as a

I smiled, realizing I was in the presence of a person who never left the seventies.

devout follower of Le Studio. In the front lot, near the stairs that led up to the studio, Richard had placed souvenir plaques firmly into the ground. These testaments bore witness to the memory of what this place meant to music, particularly Rush—the tribute space proudly represented all of Rush's discography.

Richard even started a GoFundMe campaign with hopes of restoring Le Studio for a whopping $2.4 million. Unfortunately, it was unsuccessful, only raising just under $9,000.

Even though the campaign didn't have enough capital to launch, Richard kept up the memory of Le Studio in his way. He maintained an online store of Le Studio souvenirs, selling T-shirts, hoodies, pens, and guitar picks. This sacred space showcased an oil painting of Le Studio. Richard even preserved glass bits from the recording room, encased in clear display containers. Needless to say, the studio was a special part of Richard's life and the lives of many music fans, evidenced by people still making a pilgrimage to it.

The studio overlooked a lake. Rumors were that some musicians would swim from their residential areas across the lake, right to the back of the studio, and record.

This secluded musical haven cultivated creativity.

❄ ❄ ❄

The real estate guru and I were going to buy all the land around the lake and build luxurious log cabins. I caught his vision, and it sounded glamorous. He said we would sell these homes for two million each, and we would pocket amazing profits. Later on, when I did my spreadsheets, I was floored. I realized I would make $50 million.

I had many questions. For example, the Fiddler Lake project sold cottages for $400,000 to $500,000. How exactly could we do a four-times markup? He told me it would not be a problem. He said we didn't have to worry because the market was hot. He had it figured out. We would be rich if I followed along.

Real estate wasn't my domain, so I trusted this self-declared expert. I thought he knew what he was talking about since he, supposedly, had built so many things. He told me he had done it before. Why wouldn't I trust him?

But as you might have noticed, red flags sprang up, no matter how I tried to avoid them. There were quite a few times my gut told me to get the hell out of there. One time I went to see his attorney at his office in an old decrepit building. Andy, we'll call him, gave off a weird vibe. I had to pay him fees for the deal, starting at $90,000. I balked at it internally, but I thought to myself, *You have to spend money to make money*. Besides, I had millions, and this was a drop in the bucket.

There were quite a few times my gut told me to get the hell out of there.

And that was the start of a string of fees that came my way—thousands for this and thousands for that. I didn't question anything. I thought my partner, the "guru," was leading me down the right path because I certainly couldn't. He knew much more about it than I did.

Of course, it didn't mean I was a complete fool. I knew something was happening under the surface, so I bought the studio, and the "guru" bought the other land where the cottages would be. I thought if I owned the studio in my own name, it would be my edge over him. The studio was a big part of the appeal, and it could have sold for large sums of money. It stood in front of the lake in the mountain, and the view was gorgeous.

Regrettably, the costs kept piling up, and I was the one paying all of them. The attorney fees cost a fortune. I also put down money for the plans. These were hundreds of thousands in fees. I absorbed all of the marketing and staff.

Every month, I paid $15,000 for the insurance, heating, and taxes. The marketing fees cost me $20,000 a month, and the trade shows kept on going. Expenses piled up. All of the money poured out of my accounts, bleeding like a stuck pig—because that's what I essentially was in this scenario. I was the main dish getting served up.

After being drained of all my cash, I was on the verge of bankruptcy. But I still held out hope because as soon as the cottages sold, I would make millions. I kept hanging on. I needed to make it happen.

Then the market crashed. The Great Recession hit like a freight train. Real estate values took a nosedive, and investors scurried out like rats fleeing a sinking ship.

In the summer of 2007, I went to a trade show in London to promote the project. I still thought maybe I could pull this thing off. I believed I could sell my way out of this quagmire and put some money in my pocket in the process. Maybe I could at least make back what I had spent.

By this time, it was too late. All I heard at the trade show were crickets. Only two months prior, the place was packed wall to wall.

I called my wife and told her nobody was there. At that moment, I realized I was done. It was over. I felt weak, as if my blood—my lifeforce—had rushed out of me. It was nothing I had ever experienced before or since.

Out of desperation, I called my parents—a thirty-seven-year-old man, crying.

The next six months, I sunk into a deep depression. As I watched bills stack up, I felt sharp pains in my stomach. I saw my bank account go down to nothing. Because I was down to my last dollar, I had to sell the house and then my condo. Finally, out of desperation, I called my parents—a thirty-seven-year-old man, crying.

All of this loss was because I didn't trust myself. Instead, I followed a stranger down a rabbit hole I knew nothing about.

Eventually, a lawyer bought out my shares for pennies on the dollar. I didn't care that I was smoked on the deal. I just needed to be out, so I had to take anything offered to me. Despite finding myself amid a financial tailspin, I still managed to make arrangements to pay my debts to the people I owed. I paid every single nickel back in the end.

I couldn't fathom how I managed to be so sharp with Pivotal and so foolish with Le Studio. It made little sense. I couldn't gauge what was happening, and I didn't stand up to anyone, even as I was getting stripped of my wealth day by day.

The "guru" saw me trying to get a venture going, and he took this as his opportunity to latch onto a source of cash. He reversed the pitch on me, then positioned himself as the ultimate authority.

The entire situation was fraught with warning signs. The guru's brother went to jail for fraud. His credit cards often declined. He had no furniture. I should have heeded those red flags, but I didn't. When I finally started listening, it was already too late. I was caught up way too deep in the mess.

With Pivotal, I was very knowledgeable. But with real estate, I was in over my head. I was either ignorant or prideful.

But this experience also allowed me to see how dangerous storytelling can be. That's all the guru was: a brilliant storyteller. He painted any picture he imagined, and he projected that picture vividly to others. I still look back on that nightmare and get shivers.

Besides, I wasn't the right person for the Le Studio opportunity. I only knew the fact that a few big names used to record their songs there. Le Studio deserved someone with a passion for music and the cultural value it represented. It should have been in the hands of someone who understood the value of the history made there.

I failed, and it was time for me to pack my bags. I felt far from lucky, and, for a while, that seemed to be the end of the story for me. Thankfully, stories can change without any warning.

4

Second Wind

For what it's worth: it's never too late or, in my case,
too early to be whoever you want to be. There's no time
limit; stop whenever you want. You can change or stay
the same; there are no rules to this thing. We can make
the best or the worst of it. I hope you make the best of it.
And I hope you see things that startle you. I hope you feel
things you never felt before. I hope you meet people who
have a different point of view. I hope you live a life you're
proud of. If you find that you're not, I hope you have the
strength to start all over again.
—F. Scott Fitzgerald,
The Curious Case of Benjamin Button

I n the summer of 2008, I sat in my home office staring
at a stack of envelopes. My computer displayed my bank
portal. With each envelope I opened, an electric shock
jolted through my stomach. I couldn't believe how much I

owed. I gathered the bills in a pile and felt their intimidating weight. I didn't want to calculate the total. Would I have anything left? A lump formed in my throat, like a massive gumball—it grew in size each time I opened a new bill.

When I look back to those periods, I can only think of them as dark days. I had never experienced that kind of thing before. It felt like someone draped a curtain over my head and blinded me. I forgot who I was.

I had been many things in my life at that point—an executive, an entrepreneur, a sports agent, but, most of all, a hard worker who always found a way. This was how my parents raised me, and I prided myself on that fact.

For a while, all of that went out the window, and I was a shell of my former self. Those days blurred together. Each time I checked my bank account, I felt more stress and anxiety.

> **All of that went out the window, and I was a shell of my former self.**

I don't exactly know how I woke up from that daze. My body and mind felt paralyzed. Even when I was bought out and exited that business, I still felt low. The depression lasted for months afterward.

Some say depression affects your ability to think critically and renders you incapable of proper problem-solving. This was definitely the case with me. I drifted and allowed the current of life to simply take me and wash me down the hole of failure. Days, weeks, and months went on like that when I just thought, *This is it. It's over.*

One day out of the blue, I woke up and thought to myself, *I gotta do something. I can't just wither away and die.* Maybe my body knew I was giving up, and a survival instinct kicked in. I felt a strong urge to battle my way out of this.

Suddenly, everything became clearer. Next, I made a few phone calls in the hopes that someone could help me out. It was not much of a plan, but I did it anyway. The financial fortress I had built for myself crumbled. All I had left were my connections.

Then it happened. I called one of my friends, Todd Whiton, and told him straight that I needed his help, that I was on the verge of bankruptcy. I laid out the whole story, from start to finish, of how I was practically ruined at this point.

He couldn't believe it, and I don't think anyone would have believed it. One moment I was heading into the sunset with a bag of cash, ready to fly into a new horizon, and the next moment I was sending out an SOS—dead broke.

"I need to get my confidence back. I don't feel like a man anymore, and mostly I need cash."

He said, "Well, you may have called at the right time. My friend's company just struck a deal with a large Canadian bank, and they are looking for an investor, somebody to bring some money to the table and take an ownership stake and to run the company for them."

My ears perked up right then, and I knew I could do something. There was only one problem. I didn't have any money. I let out a laugh once I realized that, perhaps the first time that I had laughed in months.

"That's great, Todd, but I don't have a penny to my name."

> I didn't have any money. I let out a laugh once I realized that, perhaps the first time that I had laughed in months.

"Listen to me," he said. "I'll get you a phone call with them, and you will figure that out later."

That was how I got connected to the founder of EVO Payments. EVO was a payment processing company, and they were looking for someone in Canada to get the company into the Canadian market. I must've fit like a glove because I had previous experience growing Pivotal.

I called the founder of EVO Payments and his COO, Kevin Lambrix, and somehow I found the courage to push through. I told them that I was the guy they wanted if EVO Payments would make it into the Canadian market, selling myself as much as I could on that call.

At the time, they were also negotiating with someone else, but my pitch on the phone worked. The founder and COO liked me, and we hit it off. After we'd been speaking for a couple of weeks, I flew to New York to talk in person.

I took a chance that this would be a great opportunity for me. I had butterflies in my stomach, and I was nervous as hell. But I knew I needed to make something work from this meeting.

I reminded myself who I was and what I excelled at. I was a sales guy, a brilliant one, and I knew my stuff. Since I had already made a great business come alive, I knew I could do it again. I shook off all that negative baggage I had acquired from the real estate business—the feeling that I didn't know a thing and that I was a failure. I knocked all of that out of my head.

Then I walked into their office. I don't know where I got the strength, but I mustered it together for that one moment. Right then, all my fears, my doubts, and my crippling anxiety turned into courage. Enough was enough because this was something I already was—a successful executive in the payments' business. The real estate game might have knocked the confidence out of me, but this was where I would get it all back. I reminded myself I was in my element, I was a shark, and this space was like water to me—my regular hunting ground.

Right then, all my fears, my doubts, and my crippling anxiety turned into courage.

I pitched like I was a baseball player playing my best game ever. Everything clicked. It was hands down the best pitch of my life. I practically sold my heart into this deal.

In the end, it was a success. They wanted to partner with me. I would run the Canadian division of EVO Payments and get 30 percent equity. At the time, I had nothing in my pockets, as in zero dollars. But the fact that I could somehow negotiate 30 percent equity was a huge boost of confidence to me. The catch, of course, was that I had to put $200,000 into this venture, which I definitely didn't have.

I changed my thinking immediately. I began to imagine how I could raise that money, even though I had way too much debt and couldn't turn to the banks. Plus, the economy was in tatters, and the studio property wasn't going to be of any use. So I kept my gears turning and turning until I found the boldest strategy I could think of.

I was going to raise money for a company I didn't even own yet.

This part was surprisingly simple. I knew I had a good name and reputation. I knew **I was going to raise money for a company I didn't even own yet.** people were familiar with how I had grown a business to a massive size before, particularly in the payments' industry. There were people willing to bet on my next project. I leveraged that belief. It made sense that a new payments' company in Canada would be backed by a major payments' corporation and led by the best guy possible for the position.

At the time, the Canadian payments market was a massive blue ocean. So EVO Canada was going to be one of the very first movers in the country. The conditions were right, the infrastructure around it seemed solid, and people knew my abilities already.

Of course, it wasn't easy. It's always the simple things that are the hardest to achieve. It was the middle of the recession. Many people had bled a ton of money, and I must have looked insane trying to get people to invest in a new business when I had just experienced a massive real estate failure.

But my classic work ethic kicked in then, and I just dialed everyone I knew who might have been willing to invest in me. Sure enough, it was a no after no after no, but I didn't stop. Call number twenty-five soon turned into call number forty-eight, then call number sixty-seven. I kept a record of it all. Finally, call number eight-seven clicked.

After I got one person to believe in me, things became easier. I managed to raise $300,000 for 5 percent of EVO Canada out of the shares I would get. After the money came through, I got my shares in EVO Canada as promised, and I gave a portion of those shares to my investors.

What started as a dark day turned into an amazing day almost overnight. That experience showed me that the lowest low could turn into a roaring comeback. It landed like a goal that went in to tie the game with five seconds left on the clock.

But the biggest takeaway from all of this was not that I had negotiated my way into EVO and that I had managed to sell shares in this company I didn't own yet. My biggest success came from my renewed confidence. At that moment, I took control of my life again. The downward spiral had ended.

At that moment, I took control of my life again. The downward spiral had ended.

✿ ✿ ✿

After I executed that master stroke of a deal, we launched EVO Canada in March 2009. I was the only employee.

EVO Canada started off specializing in small-to-medium-sized retail businesses. It started a bit rocky because it turns out the company was hatching another plan beneath the surface. The top brass at EVO had already invested in another payment processing company based out of Ontario.

They thought we should merge because it didn't make sense to have two Canadian companies under the same umbrella.

At the time, I thought it was a good idea. The more the merrier, right?

The head of the other company and his cofounder came to Montreal to work together to plan the launch of EVO Canada. I had already started to score quite a number of sales on my own, and I was getting in the rhythm of things.

When I picked him up at the airport, he asked me what was with all these people speaking French. Immediately, I knew I did not like this guy. He went on a tirade listing his doubts about doing business in Montreal, how English was the way to go, and how we were doing it wrong. All of this was nonsense because he didn't have an open mind.

He never understood the value of being in this region of the country—the cheaper real estate prices, the lower expected salaries. The entire time he wanted me to get out of Montreal and go elsewhere. I didn't want to leave because I already lived in Montreal and had built a large company servicing the English marketplace there.

This was when I applied a lesson I had learned from my dark days. I stood my ground. During the real estate days, I got pushed into a position where someone could take advantage of me, and I would not let that happen again. If I backed down here, not only would he drag me toward his will at every chance he got, but I would lose my self-respect too. If this happened, I would stop enjoying my work.

Therefore, I refused to stand down. I was adamant about staying in Montreal, and by association, EVO Canada was going to stay as a company based in Montreal. As a result, the merger fell through. I won out, and the leadership decided that I alone would lead EVO Canada.

When we launched right out of the gates, we had difficulty convincing any retailer to adopt us as their payment processor.

We weren't a trusted financial institution, and it's difficult to win people over when you're the new kid on the block.

I brought in the first sales in the beginning. Another colleague handled operations. Still, I knew I couldn't be the only person making the sales if we were going to go big across the market and beat out the competition. My former company Pivotal got into the Canadian market by acquiring Cardex, so I needed to move fast.

The problem was that we didn't have a huge budget to hire a salaried sales team, and there would not be any additional capital pool to do this. Hence, this is where I used a new method to our advantage.

First, we put ads everywhere we could, including newspapers and online forums, such as Craigslist. Then, we gathered all these resumes and called each of them up to register for a webinar. I told them about the business we were in, how it was profitable, and how they, as non-salaried sales executives, could make an incredible amount of money.

It was difficult to get people onboard with the webinar. Out of the first 150 conversations I had with potential applicants, only ten showed up to the first one. But out of those ten, eight joined us and agreed to start working for us with no salary. That was incredible because I did not know what to expect at first.

Despite the nature of it being a commission-only position, the story was compelling. I told them they could reach a six-figure salary as long as they did the work. I told them we would be the ones generating the leads. That was a huge part of the whole pitch. We called the merchants and asked if they'd book an appointment with a sales executive, and then we would pass these warm leads onto the commission salespeople.

Each person would get three to four appointments a day, more if they could handle it. They only needed to convince the merchants enough so they would pull the trigger. This concept of giving warm leads to a sales team was unheard of in Canada but had been successful in the US.

This recruiting method allowed us to expand our operations quickly and plant a sales executive in every corner of the country. Soon eight became almost one hundred.

The following year, things were going great at this point. I had created a well-oiled engine, and the new company was humming along beautifully.

But like many revelations I had in my life, a feeling crept up on me one day. It was almost two years after launching the company. I was working late in my office, and I was fried. My mind was numb. I looked through my email inbox, which had more than a thousand unread messages. No matter how much I worked through them, I couldn't see the bottom of it.

I looked around. I had over two hundred employees. A big number of them were sales executives situated across the country. I was involved in every decision and event in the company, even though we had become much bigger.

I was running hot, like a car about to break down. Was I driving the business, or was the business driving me? I knew the answer to the question. I was a slave to the machine I had created, being dragged along, tied at the wrist.

Was I driving the business, or was the business driving me?

Most of all, I knew I was losing interest. I couldn't continue like this. Even though I was running a great company and had amazing employees, I didn't feel like I had accomplished much. I should have felt like a rockstar. But I didn't.

That's when I decided I'd hit a wall. I needed someone to teach me how to be better. I needed guidance. I needed a coach. But where would I find one?

5

A Change of Pace

Change is never a matter of ability;
it's always a matter of motivation.
—Tony Robbins

Until I had gone to EVO Canada, I had made my own decisions. There was no guidance coming from anyone, and I moved through life on instinct.

But my time at EVO Canada revealed something profound. I needed help. Despite everything working out, I was not exactly in the best place. I managed to dig myself out from the dark hole of defeat, and I was poised for financial greatness once again, this time on more stable footing. Yet I was not satisfied with my life. I was unhealthy, mentally exhausted, and I felt like a string stretched beyond its limits.

Around that time, I started listening to Tony Robbins again. My father had introduced me to him when he was educating us about self-development.

During my days of depression, my wife and I were watching a Tony Robbins video, and I distinctly remember telling her I would meet him one day. Maybe it was a hope kindling in my mind that meeting him would solve my problems.

When I decided to pursue coaching, Tony Robbins immediately came to my mind. He had a program called the Tony Robbins Business Mastery taking place in Las Vegas in January. It was a five-day event, and they'd structured the whole thing around breaking down every aspect of your business and teaching you how to optimize each element.

The ticket for the Business Mastery Event was $10,000, yet despite my new success with EVO Canada, I was recovering from being dead broke. I still had bills I needed to pay from that grand failure. The ticket was expensive, but I knew it would be worth it.

This was the first time I had ever been to something like this, and I immediately loved it. The energy was off the charts. People were pumped, and everyone was there for one person: Tony Robbins.

The event was a series of five two-hour sessions every day. It started at 8:00 a.m., then went to around five or six in the evening. Leading each session was an expert who did a deep dive into every aspect of a business, such as finance, sales, legal, and marketing. For example, Chet Holmes, the author of *The Ultimate Sales Machine*, led the sales session. Tony had one of his best CFO buddies unpack balance sheets and financial statements for the accounting session.

The best part of these sessions was when Tony picked two or three people from the audience. He engaged them about their business, then told them what was wrong with it and how they could optimize it. Naturally, I wanted to be one of these people.

During a session on sales funnels, I saw my opportunity. I'd built a sales organization, after all. I had telemarketers booking appointments for my sales reps on the road. Then the sales reps would go in, pitch, make the sale, then follow with an upsell. I had essentially built an intricate sales funnel.

Before the session, I asked the coach who had signed me up for the course how I could be the one who gets picked. I didn't want to leave it up to chance. I wanted to stack the odds in my favor and create my own luck.

He told me if I wanted Tony to talk to me, I only had to do one thing—stand up at the beginning of the session. He said to keep standing and never sit down. I thought this was a crazy suggestion. The place was packed with thousands of people. But he was adamant.

The session started, and the crowd was pumped. There were thousands in the auditorium. And I just went with it. I stood up. Tony presented on stage, explaining the value of a sales funnel and unpacking every aspect of it, talking about how if you tweak it by tiny percentages, you're going to grow your business exponentially.

All of this time, I stood. I felt like an idiot—people burning holes into the back of my head with their eyes, probably thinking to themselves, "Who the hell is this bald guy randomly standing up?"

Who the hell is this bald guy randomly standing up?

Thinking back, I must have looked like someone who was throwing some kind of wild prank. My tenacity was rewarded when Tony stopped and asked me, "Sir, how can I help you?"

And I give him a straight answer. "I want to be the guy you interview."

So he said, "What business are you in?"

"I'm in credit card processing," I said.

He asked me the same question again. It was several days into the course, and one of the things he had taught us was that we're often not in the business we think we're in.

So I quickly changed course. I told him I was in the business of maximizing my client's profits, and Tony enjoyed that response much more.

"NICE!" he yelled in his signature raspy baritone voice.

That started one of the most memorable conversations I've ever had in my life. I stood in the audience talking to Tony while he stood on the stage.

For the next forty-five minutes or so, we began an exchange that went into every aspect of the sales funnel of my business. We talked about how many potential customers were in my database, how I could increase the number of clients I reach, and how to convert them better. It was a fantastic brainstorming session. We went back and forth, and I came prepared. For every question Tony threw out, I had an answer ready, which kept the flow of the conversation going. It was blistering. Tony moved fast, and I kept up with him.

By the time we were done, I got a standing ovation from everyone. After the session, people swarmed me, giving me their business cards to partner with me. They asked when we were going public because they wanted to get in on my company's shares when we did. I ended up with hundreds of business cards. I felt incredible.

Having thoroughly seen what it was like being coached by Tony Robbins, I decided to join his platinum partner group at the conference. This group was his version of a mastermind, and it opened up a lot of exclusive access to his private events and coaching opportunities. The only problem was that the price tag was $65,000! I had just spent $10,000, and now I was about to spend more than six times that amount.

I knew I had to find a way to fund this next-level group. There were many benefits to joining this group other than the exclusive trips and the coaching. There was also an incredible network. I reasoned that the people in this group would have paid the same as me, which meant a good network of committed businesspeople, each with a high net worth. Not anyone could pay $65,000 to get into the group. Sure enough, I made some valuable connections through this group, two that would even lead to other profitable ventures down the line.

All in all, the experience completely transformed me and my business. I came back from that conference fired up. I followed Tony's blueprint and did major restructuring, replacing all of the leaders in the organization that were not right for their positions. As a result, sales went up 30 percent.

But that was not the main takeaway from the conference. What I gained from the Tony Robbins event was much more. I experienced renewed energy—a shot of vitality directly into my veins.

I learned one more important thing—if the business was failing, it was my fault. If business stressed me out, it was my fault. The whole session made me aware of how my shortcomings resulted in the negative outcomes I had experienced.

I went about addressing this. I took myself off a vast majority of email lists. Before then, I would get hundreds of emails in my inbox daily, and I felt overwhelmed. But I reduced this down to around thirty. That saved me time and mental energy to do more important things.

I also realized how important it was to be around positive people. These people might have been richer and smarter, but, even more importantly, they had the right kind of mindset and perspective about life.

Jim Rohn once said that we are the average of the five people we spend the most time with, which was definitely the case for me. After just a few days with these people, I turned into a completely different person. This principle was proven to me once again several months after they invited me to the platinum partners trip in Sun Valley, Idaho.

Tony took us to a select location, where we would have an amazing time. We'd also be surrounded by some of the most elite businesspeople from around the world.

We'd wake up in the morning, do Tai Chi for an hour, then we'd board a bus to go skiing until 1:00 p.m. Later, we'd go to the conference room for coaching sessions.

Skiing proved to be one of the most memorable parts. They broke us into small groups with a private ski instructor attached to each of us. These instructors were amazing. Until then, I considered myself a decent skier, but I was an expert after being coached by the instructor that week. I skied black diamonds and powder in no time at all.

But the best part, hands down, was the network. Hanging out with wealthy business executives had already given me more financial security. They instilled in me the type of mindset I'd need to continue being successful. Hence, my experiences with Tony Robbins whetted my appetite for personal development, and I began to look more actively for business coaching from then on.

The next person I chose as a coach was Dan Sullivan, founder and president of Strategic Coach. His 10X Group focuses on optimizing your business for exponential growth. Our quarterly workshops took place at his main office in Toronto. At these meetings, I gained a ton of knowledge about management tactics I hadn't learned before.

Of course, the network was once again solid. I was probably the poorest guy there, despite being a CEO of a large payments' company. Flanked by billionaires on my left and right, I engaged in elevated conversations that continued to help me grow. The knowledge I gained in these conversations was priceless, and I knew right away it was money well spent to continue my journey in personal development.

Dan taught me a tremendous lesson on the importance of delegating. He coined the concept of a self-managing business, in which all you have to do is just put the right people in the right places, and the company would run itself while you focus on what you want to do.

He coined the concept of a self-managing business. Dan pounded this idea—that we should simply do what we're best at and get rid of everything else from our plate by creating a particular environment and structure. Delegate to the right people, then trust them to take over that part.

By doing so, I could free up the mental space to do what matters. This particular lesson impacted me significantly because this was the precise thing I struggled with right before I started pursuing coaching. Learning how to free up the mental space holding me back would declutter my mind and allow me to be a more effective leader. This would take me to the next level because it would allow me to focus on the important things—the things that move the needle.

Richard Branson, founder of the Virgin Group, embodied this particular lesson in a way I had hoped to implement in my own business. With hundreds of companies in his control, he ensured he had the appropriate personnel placed in those companies while he focused on the big picture of the entire Virgin Group.

Despite the costs involved, engaging in these programs by Tony Robbins and Dan Sullivan turned everything around for me. I got better at managing my business and gained knowledge about specific parts of running a company. Overall, it was like the MBA I never received.

Most importantly, I gained the awareness and permission to focus on myself. Until I discovered the world of self-development, I ran everywhere chasing after the money. After my experience with Le Studio, I realized the focus of my efforts should be about making me a better person every day, not simply acquiring more dollars. No wonder I felt so fried a few years into EVO! I was a hamster caught in a wheel, not knowing where to go but forced to keep running.

The coaching and mentoring allowed me to organize my mind to create my future, one in which I felt happy and satisfied.

I thank Tony and Dan for the gifts they brought me. Without them, I wouldn't have experienced all the luck that started to come my way.

6

New Horizons

If happiness is the goal—and it should be—the
adventures should be top priority.
—Richard Branson

When EVO Canada started in 2009, the banks were
practically robbing their customers because they
had no competition. They charged a merchant a
credit card processing fee of around 5 percent per transaction.
For example, a restaurant owner would pay five dollars to the
bank for a one-hundred-dollar meal. We thought this was
theft for the services they provided.

As a result, it was easy to cut their costs by more than half,
making credit card transactions less costly for any merchant.
This was how we crushed our competition in the beginning. The margins were fat. We literally stole market share
away from the banks by the truckload. The only other serious competitor was Cardex, owned by Pivotal. This meant,

in the beginning, there was plenty of space for us to grow exponentially.

But then I learned something else pretty quickly. Pricing was never a good defensive strategy. Once you start the pricing game, there's no end to it. It's a race to the bottom.

Unfortunately, we didn't have any other advantages that another competitor couldn't easily copy. For example, we didn't have any technology that was a marked improvement that would take another company years to catch up to. Once people saw us doing well, we had copycats coming into the market from all corners. This competition started to eat into our bottom line.

And then the banks gradually woke up to the sea of change happening around them. The payment processing industry was a margins game, and as soon as the big banks decided they would be serious about that part of the playing field, it was done. Margins compressed very quickly.

On top of that, in 2013, I realized the market for payment processing in Canada was not growing at the same rate. From where I stood, I could see we had essentially peaked as a payment processing business. We had to look at another way of generating profits or sell the ship.

We started doing things like building websites and online marketing for clients. But the margins on them were not that great, and the cancellation rate was high. The business was beginning to run out of steam, so some hard decisions had to be made quickly.

Around that time, EVO Payments International appointed a new CEO. I told him that I sensed the winds changing and we needed to get the hell out of the Canadian market because competitors were willing to buy us for great multiples. We were at the height of our valuation, and from here on out, we would have to fight an extremely difficult battle for every share of the pie. This was the obvious choice. We needed to exit.

But to my surprise, he refused to even entertain the thought of selling the company. He said we couldn't possibly sell it because they needed the Canadian story of EVO. It was an essential part of the North American operation of the mother company. With the signs so obviously there, this seemed irrational to me. The alarm bells were ringing—this was the ideal time to get out. I didn't need a crystal ball to see it, and I'm certain the new CEO noticed that as well.

That's the thing about running things not entirely yours. Running businesses that don't belong to you 100 percent, or at least 51 percent, presents all kinds of challenges. In the end, I was ultimately at the mercy of the mothership company, EVO Payments International. I did not know this at the time, but there was a bigger play at hand. They were lining up the entire EVO corporation to go public, and they needed the Canadian story because they wanted to flex their muscles as a global company.

I felt stuck. I knew nobody would buy me out, and they didn't want to sell the company. I repeatedly tried to convince them the market was at the top, but of course, no one listened.

I repeatedly tried to convince them the market was at the top, but of course, no one listened.

Without much of a choice, I hunkered down for the next three years and did my best, but once I decided that this was it, I was done. My eyes floated elsewhere.

I'm someone who prides himself on being accountable, and that came first and foremost in the matters of EVO Canada. As a partner, I had to be responsible for the company's well-being, for my shareholders, and for the employees. Whether I was stuck or not, I still made great money and owned 30 percent of a very valuable company. However, I was not convinced the value would hold over time. So I looked to diversify my investments into other areas.

One key domain I was interested in was the fitness industry. Until my forties, I thought I was in good shape. But that all changed when I stepped on a body composition scale. I was disgusted by what I saw—an overweight body, with my visceral fat level at ten. In addition, I had 23 percent body fat, and my metabolic age was fifty-two. (The safe zone is ten years younger than your chronological age). This horrified me, and I realized I needed to get in shape and take back control of my body.

Naturally, I started researching fitness and nutrition. I met Stephan in Sun Valley, Idaho, during the platinum event with Tony Robbins. We connected at the event, and he also turned out to be from Montreal. We became good friends. Our conversations went to fitness and nutrition, and I found out he was making an amazing amount of recurring revenue from his nutrition business.

It was a multi-level marketing brand, and at first I scoffed at it because these things reminded me of pyramid schemes. These were the businesses people went into and most often *lost* money instead of making any. Stephan, however, implemented some different ideas in his business model. He wanted to prove to me what he was doing was unique and that it worked.

He offered to fly me out to LA and show me how to combine fitness and nutrition to create a great business. At that point, I had nothing to lose. Despite my distaste for multi-level marketing, I was impressed by the amount of money he was making compared to the efforts he was putting in. Besides, at a minimum, at least I could enjoy LA.

The business model Stephan showed me was something pioneered by another gentleman by the name of Mark. He would host free boot camps on the beach. Then, after the workout, he would invite the participants back to his nutrition club to teach them about post-workout nutrition. This was how he monetized his business.

Stephan flew me out, and I brought my personal trainer with me as well. Again, I needed a domain expert to inform my decisions. My trainer and I thought we'd just glance over it, then go out to Santa Monica Pier, visit a bar, or hang out on the beach. We wanted to enjoy the West Coast—and we had nothing to lose.

When we arrived at Santa Monica Beach, where the boot camp took place, we were stunned. It was amazing. Music pumped through the air, and we saw hundreds of young people in great shape and high energy participating. I couldn't believe my eyes. I almost died during the beach workout session, keeling over with exhaustion at the end of it.

> **Music pumped through the air, and we saw hundreds of young people in great shape and high energy participating.**

However, the truly phenomenal thing was that when the boot camp was over, they invited everyone to get their post-workout protein shakes at a nutrition club in Culver City, almost half an hour drive away in Los Angeles traffic. When I heard that, I thought no one would show up. No shake was worth a thirty-minute drive.

When I arrived, I shook my head in disbelief. I figured close to 70 percent of the people on the beach had gotten into their cars and went back to the nutrition club. It didn't compute for me.

At the club, everyone got their shakes, and I saw that it wasn't just an after-workout shake session. At this large gathering, people told stories about how much weight they lost and how much better they felt. They didn't feel anxiety any longer, and they managed to eliminate their depression.

Many of the attendees were distributors. They shared about how much they made as distributors and what they did to grow their incomes. People were full of energy from the workout and pumped with optimism and positivity from all the stories.

I saw the genius of it right away. Essentially, the guy had cracked the code for selling his goods by bringing athletics into the business. First, people got pumped up by working out during the boot camp; then, they would go back to the club for a shake, where someone would pitch the nutrition supplements.

The final kicker?

The average client would stay on the nutrition program for months or even years. So if you put together hundreds, or even thousands, of these clients, that meant a hefty amount of recurring revenue.

My mind perked up. I had to get something similar going in Montreal. When I came back from LA, I told my wife, and she immediately loved the idea. I would invest the capital because I couldn't commit any time while I was still at EVO. My wife decided to run the business.

Unfortunately, we don't have a beach in Montreal, and it gets very cold and snowy in the winter. She couldn't just run a boot camp anywhere. We knew we needed to find a space and turn it into a fitness studio. This way, people wouldn't have to drive to get their shakes and hear the stories. We could do it all in the same place.

She did just that. She started looking for locations. It was going to be a nutrition club in the front and a workout area in the back.

During this time, I coached my wife on all aspects of building a business, from marketing and sales to putting together a rock-solid team. Finally, a real estate agent friend found a location for the business, and I went to check it out. I wanted to make sure it was money well invested.

The spacious location was above a Royal Bank of Canada branch on a corner. Something wasn't right, and when we did a sound test, I realized there was a language school above the space. Our boot camps would blare music on full blast late in the evening. This wouldn't work.

Finally, there was an opening on the second floor of my building, and I suggested the team consider it. I thought to myself: *This would be perfect because I could go work out whenever I wanted.* It took about four months to get that place ready, and while it was being built, the serious recruiting began. We showed everybody what we were building to help them visualize it as much as possible.

The company formally launched in April 2013, and the business took off like a rocket ship. The business grew from one location to twenty-five locations across Canada. I enjoyed watching this growth while still at EVO. I felt like I got these small hits of excitement that come from entrepreneurship.

> **I got these small hits of excitement that come from entrepreneurship.**

❄ ❄ ❄

Before EVO went on the public markets, I figured they would probably want to get all the minority shareholders out, and that included me with my 30 percent, which was quite a chunk. When that opportunity came up, I was determined to make the most of this. Remembering the disastrous real estate failure I had experienced, I vowed I would come out on top. As a result, I hired a brilliant lawyer, Keith Wilson, for the negotiation.

My lawyer had some great insights about what EVO's next moves would be. At the time, it still was not clear that EVO would debut on the market, but my lawyer looked at the company landscape and determined EVO was positioning itself to go public. He made a judgment call that, based on that leverage, we could get the most value out of my shares.

His decision was spot on. With my shares in the balance, my lawyer and I dragged the negotiations out for months. At this point, with the assumption they were indeed going public, time was on my side, and we stayed patient as my lawyer guided me through the process. I'm still with him today, and he continues to do great work for me. It pays dividends to be with people you trust to do good work for you in the long term. As a result, in 2016, I successfully exited from EVO Canada with a very comfortable amount of cash.

This was the fourth and final payments' company I was involved in, and the end of my time at EVO marked an end of an era for me that spanned nearly two decades. It was a good time to leave though. I grew as much as I could, and my mind and body craved a new adventure. Unfortunately, staying in the payments' business wasn't going to do that for me.

❧ ❧ ❧

When I came out of EVO, I decided to go full-time in the fitness business. For a while, I made that my main focus, but it did not take long for me to spot another opportunity.

At the time, I was doing much of the marketing. This involved buying paid ads on Facebook, and I never enjoyed doing this. So I began to look for someone else to take over the marketing side of things. If someone could beat my cost per lead, they could have the job.

If someone could beat my cost per lead, they could have the job.

Over the course of that year, I hired several marketing professionals and agencies to try and beat my numbers. I did not consider myself a skilled media buyer, yet I had crushed everyone who came up to the challenge.

Finally, I was introduced to a gentleman named Max. He beat my numbers by a wide margin. I made good on my promise and hired him to advertise the fitness centers on social media.

After working with him for six months, I saw a new business in the making. Max had such a talent for this that I thought to myself, *If I'm benefiting from this, there must be tons of other businesses that could benefit from this as well.* Heck, there was a business somewhere in there.

This was the beginning of our new company together— Maxy Media. Luckily, at the time, I could step away from the fitness centers because they were making good recurring revenue, and the business was in great hands. In addition, my wife was doing a phenomenal job.

I became the CEO of this new company as someone with more business experience and as someone who could counterbalance the passionate energy Max had as a young inexperienced founder.

The business grew quickly, and we were profitable right out of the gate. The thirst for Facebook advertising was a felt need in the marketplace, so we could sell our services as Facebook media buyers for dozens of companies.

We also did native advertising, which involved buying advertising space that looked like organic content on media websites. This was another space killing it around the time we launched.

It wasn't all easy, though, and whenever we thought we had figured something out, we were thrown a curveball. For instance, Facebook shut us down twice. The first time it happened, we just refocused on native advertising. Then it happened again, and we realized we needed to diversify badly.

That was when TikTok emerged.

TikTok started exploding around 2019, and it grew at a breakneck speed. We dove into TikTok right when their ad platform launched. We were early on the scene—literally at the start.

Unlike advertising on any other platform, media buying on TikTok was a difficult endeavor. Ad fatigue on TikTok is short compared to other media platforms. So ad campaigns become ineffective very quickly.

This is where we came in with the expertise we had accumulated with Facebook. Thanks to our incredible team and our brilliant COO, Jack Antaki, we instantly shot up as the number one TikTok advertiser in terms of daily spend in Canada.

Our goal was to be a well-diversified media buying behemoth with its hands in Facebook, Snapchat, and emerging platforms, and that same goal stands today. In addition, we also aim to become the premier TikTok advertising agency. I believe this is the way we can truly thrive in this disruptive space of social media advertising. We're diversifying, but we're also building upon our strengths.

Currently, we integrate strategies no other company in the space is even thinking of doing. We want to retain our market lead, which means always looking ahead into the future. One of these strategies is building a software tool that addresses a huge weakness in TikTok's advertising platform.

I'm determined to turn this into a billion-dollar business. As of now, Maxy Media is on a path to hyper-growth. The market is expanding at a blistering pace. We're growing our team from its modest size of seventy to at least ten times that in the near future. We're poised for the kind of explosive upward trajectory that few blessed startups go through.

When I look back on my life, I can identify what I did wrong in each stage. I can pinpoint all the areas in which I made mistakes and what I should have done differently. But the only reason why I know better now is all because of the perspectives and the lessons I gained each one of those times. Every single blunder I made along the way had to happen. Otherwise, I don't think I would have gained the knowledge I have now.

In the beginning, I chased things for very superficial reasons. I went into the agent business because of the glamour it seemed to bring. It revealed how everything comes with a price. I went into the payments' business because it seemed to yield recurring revenue. I took far too many risks but, in the end, they all led me to where I am today.

Each time I took a misstep, I didn't just curse and stomp the ground. Instead, I took it as an opportunity to improve myself and go higher. As a result, these failures became steppingstones to build me into who I am now.

These failures became steppingstones to build me into who I am now.

Of course, I don't believe you should try and collect as many failures as possible. But for your life to progress, it's important to recognize what can be learned from each error you make, no matter how large or small. Failures sharpen us and foster growth as long as we let them. Even the worst times have their role in molding us into better people.

When my best client fired me as a sports agent, I found opportunities in the payments' industry. When the dot-com bubble destroyed my paper net worth, Pivotal recruited me. And when I had literally lost almost everything I owned in that real estate deal, I forged a new path with EVO Canada. Even from my worst defeat, I found a way to rise again to fight another day.

If you want a takeaway, I'll offer you one—it's never over.
Every time you think it's over, life gives you another opportunity. Believe you can make it through. After all, today might just be your lucky day.

PART 2

The Formula

If you haven't received your Lucky Score,
we suggest doing so before reading
Part 2. Take The Lucky Formula Assessment
at TheLuckyFormula.com

7

Right Conditions

Don't wait for the right opportunity. Create it.
—George Bernard Shaw

I believe in luck.

I also believe luck isn't something you get without any real effort. Luck happens when you take advantage of a force bigger than yourself. It has to do with making your actions count. Most people do things without maximizing the gains that come from their actions. I'm not exhorting you to make every day count. I'm not advocating for some crazy daily lifehacking rituals where each microsecond is exhaustively extracted for productivity. Not even close.

Luck is a force. Think of it like electricity. It's wild, full of energy, and it can be destructive. But if you harness its power, you can do anything.

When you're lucky, you can go where you want to go.

If you harness its power, you can do anything.

Most people hear the word "luck" and think about big lottery winners. This isn't luck. The actual winning part is a freak accident.

Luck is when you have a business and an objective to dominate in your industry. Because of a certain tailwind, you now find yourself in a mode of hypergrowth. For a more concrete example, take a look at the case of Zoom, the communications technology company that specializes in online conferencing services. Since it debuted on the stock market in 2019, Zoom languished for a year along with other start-ups on the public markets, like Uber and Slack. But then the COVID-19 pandemic hit, and what happened? Zoom went from around $67 a share at the beginning of the year to a whopping $500 a share in a matter of ten months. Could Eric Yuan, the founder of Zoom, predict this would happen—that a global pandemic would sweep the world and force everyone to avoid interacting with one another in person? No. But it sure helped him and his business.

Luck is never the initiator of great things, but it's often a catalyst. Wise people take advantage of a lucky situation. They don't wait for luck to fall into their laps.

Before we unpack The Lucky Formula in detail, it's important to understand what I refer to as The 3 Constants. These are nonnegotiable. Without them, the formula won't work.

Constant 1: Hard Work is Essential

You won't get far consistently without hard work. It's impossible. Talent helps. Riding on someone else's coattails creates movement. Coasting might produce some progress. But nothing yields sustainable results without hard work. It's as necessary as breathing. Bottom line: The Lucky Formula works best with hard work.

Constant 2: Learn from your Mistakes

It is okay to make mistakes. I can't think of anyone who became successful without failing. In fact, failing results from risking, and without risk, success doesn't show its face.

I've failed many times. Part 1 proves that. But I extracted an invaluable lesson with each failure. I'd apply that lesson to the next situation I faced. This is how I created bigger and bigger successes down the line. All of those lessons became steppingstones that helped me cross the chasm of complacency and into the land of success. Remember, though—no one achieves anything by making the same mistake over and over again. Learn from your mistakes.

Constant 3: Get a Clear Destination

Many people fall short because they don't have a clear goal. They don't know what to do with the opportunities in front of them. Once you get clear on where you want to go and why you want to get there, it's much easier to arrive at your intended destination.

With those three constants in mind, The Lucky Formula is quite simple to understand. The doing part? That's more difficult. It requires conscious effort. Like all formulas, it's made up of certain components, in this case, two.

Right Conditions + Right Actions = Lucky

Right conditions can be further divided into two parts: internal conditions and external conditions.

Internal Conditions + External Conditions = Right Conditions

Therefore, The Lucky Formula is best understood as follows:

Internal Conditions + External Conditions + Right Actions = Lucky

or

IC + EC + RA = Lucky

To help visualize The Lucky Formula, I've integrated the right conditions into a paradigm I refer to as The Lucky Coin©. As you incorporate each of these conditions in your life, you stack the odds in your favor. Keep stacking the odds and you'll be able to cash in on success.

EXTERNAL & INTERNAL CONDITIONS

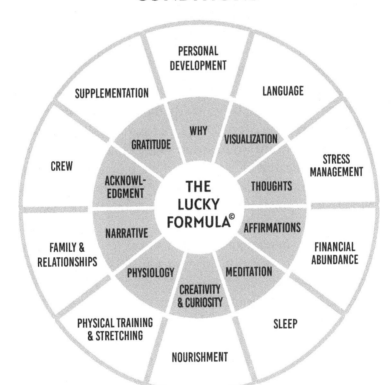

Although The Lucky Formula might feel a little abstract at the moment, in Part 2, we'll break the components down one at a time. It will soon make more sense. For now, just take notice of what I mean by conditions. I'll explain with a story.

Around the beginning of 2020, I noticed how the markets took a dive, and everyone was looking for a way to store away their money in alternative investments. Having bought gold as my hedge against such volatility, I didn't lose much. Gold went up during this time, reclaiming its classic role as a safe-haven investment vehicle.

Then the central banks started to pump money into the economy at a furious rate, and the overall money supply gave people anxiety that inflation would go through the roof. Cash would lose its value. By the end of the summer of 2020, equities were overvalued. Gold started to lose its sheen as an alternative investment and gradually dropped in price throughout the year. There was no place for money to go at this time. The stimulus kept making cash less valuable, the markets were in turmoil, and even gold and other valuable minerals weren't viable.

I read the market and decided to bet on cryptocurrency. The conditions were ripe for money to flow into these asset classes. I was right.

Conditions determine outcomes. Often people think the right conditions are random, like a manager who somehow inherits a star-studded team and is endowed with an infinite budget.

Conditions determine outcomes.

But the truth is that often, we can actually engineer what we consider right conditions, provided enough work and care goes into creating them.

Take a company's culture, for example. The people within the organization establish it. They can create a positive culture or a negative one, and, depending upon their choice, productivity increases or decreases.

Or consider the human body. A healthy, fit body allows us to do many things, including going on a long hike or working on an important project for an extended period. If we don't take care of our bodies, however, simply walking up the stairs might become difficult.

The conditions surrounding us dramatically affect us. For example, I was blessed with the condition of having two brothers play professional hockey when I started as an agent. Through my brothers, I benefitted from an easy head start on my career.

On the flip side, I was cursed by the conditions of the Great Recession when the real estate market tanked. It left me penniless. Conditions influence us positively and negatively.

Once I learned how to influence the conditions *surrounding me* and *within me*, I started optimizing them for the best outcomes. Suddenly the opportunities flowed. I had flipped my luck. One day I was down in the dumps, and the next day I became the luckiest guy I knew. And I kept getting lucky.

Eventually, it clicked. It wasn't my fortunes that had suddenly turned for the better. Rather, I created conditions that enabled me to leverage opportunities and fortunes as they came my way.

Certain conditions you can't control, like the family you're born into. My family valued work ethic. My father put me to work during high school so I could pay off my college fees. From early on, I knew the benefits of hard work, which still defines who I am today.

This was something completely outside of my control. I didn't choose to be born into that family. I can't imagine how I would have turned out if I was born into another kind of family—a rich one, for example. Would I have worked as hard if everything was simply handed to me? I doubt it.

❉ ❉ ❉

Conditions can be divided into two different kinds—internal conditions and external conditions. Internal conditions are driven by you and do not require interaction with others. External conditions require you to establish a collaborative relationship with other people.

Internal conditions can be further divided into two parts—body and mind. Both are fully within your power to influence. Despite how much other people can affect your body and your mind, you are the main driver. You decide almost everything that happens to your body—how you eat, how you move, or how you don't move.

Despite how much other people can affect your body and your mind, you are the main driver.

You also have the ability to control your mind. This is an incredible gift and power, yet many people forget this and just let themselves go. They allow themselves to be influenced by others. In such cases, you rarely get lucky. Even if an ideal opportunity presents itself, you won't take it because your mind is overtaken by somebody else's goal.

❉ ❉ ❉

External conditions are equally significant. No matter what you do in life, you have to do it with other people, especially if you want to have a successful life. The more constructive your culture, the more luck you will draw to yourself.

If someone has a great idea destined to be the next billion-dollar business, they won't share that idea with a back-stabbing pessimist. On the other hand, that person will most likely share the idea with someone who is positive, who gives credit where it's due, and who motivates others.

This is why having the right conditions is critical. It not only welcomes luck but it also sets you up for the best possible outcome. Conditions are one-half of this formula. Time and time again in my career, it felt like luck just dropped into my lap. But the more appropriate metaphor is that I made a net, cast it as far as the eye could see, and caught luck as it came.

INTERNAL CONDITIONS

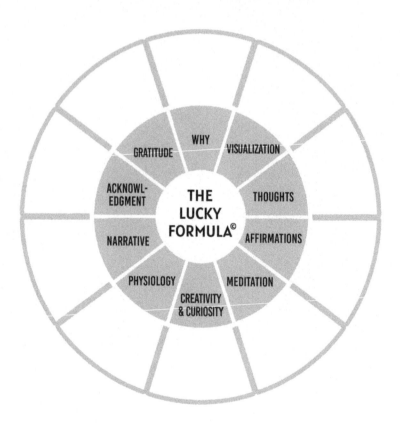

8

Internal Conditions

You will never have a greater or lesser dominion than that
over yourself. You can gauge the height of a man's success
by his self-mastery, the depth of his failure by his self-
abandonment. And this law is the expression of eternal
justice. He who cannot establish dominion over himself
will have no dominion over others.
—Leonardo da Vinci

Success in attracting luck is an internal job. It's not
something we achieve. It's someone we become. This is
why we must start with the internal conditions before
we focus on the external ones.

The Lucky Formula diagram reveals ten internal components. We'll unpack them one at a time. Let's begin with the
first one: Why.

INTERNAL CONDITIONS

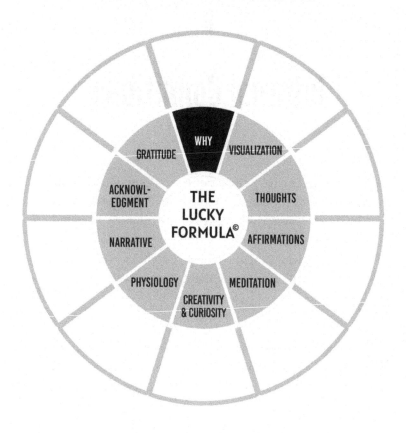

Why

Author Simon Sinek wisely advised us to *Start with Why*. In his book, named after the same exhortation, he reveals most people start with the What or the How. As a result, they fail to communicate conviction. This blurb on Amazon reveals more:

> Sinek starts with a fundamental question: Why are some people and organizations more innovative, influential, and profitable than others? Why do some command greater loyalty from customers and employees alike? Even among the successful, why are so few able to repeat their success over and over?
>
> People like Martin Luther King Jr., Steve Jobs, and the Wright Brothers had little in common, but they all started with *why*. They realized that people wouldn't truly buy into a product, service, movement, or idea until they understand the WHY behind it.
>
> *Start with Why* shows that the leaders who've had the greatest influence in the world all think, act, and communicate the same way—and it's the opposite of what everyone else does. Sinek calls this powerful idea The Golden Circle. It provides a framework upon which organizations can be built, movements can be led, and people can be inspired. And it all starts with *why*.[1]

Sinek's predecessor Friedrich Nietzsche, a German philosopher from the late 1800s, said, "He who has a *why* to live for can bear almost any *how*."[2]

The point is that our why functions as our GPS. Without a clear one, we drift aimlessly along the surface. Luck doesn't favor aimlessness. I know this firsthand. All I need to do is remember my season of depression from Part 1. Back then, I suffered from depression because I didn't know my why.

I love what Gail Hyatt says: "People lose their way when they lose their why."[3] She's right. My why was taken from me with those bad business deals, and, as a result, I lost my way.

Maybe you can relate? If so, don't despair. You can rediscover your why, and when you do, you'll also rediscover your way. When this occurs, you let luck know you're ready for a visit. It's simple, but absolutely true. I've benefited from this formula more times than I can count.

> **You can rediscover your why, and when you do, you'll also rediscover your way.**

What is your why? What is your burning reason for working so hard, for putting in the effort to attain luck? There are two ways to identify your why. The first strategy is positive. Ask yourself what gets you out of bed in the morning. Your answer might be your family, parents, close friends, or even pets. Some of my friends' why is to retire their parents. One of my whys is my family. I work hard, and I am passionate about what I do because I want my family to have an incredible life!

The second strategy to find your why is negative. Ask yourself what you absolutely hate. What gives you a visceral negative gut reaction? What do you detest deep within your core? As I discussed in Part 1, one of my whys is to never, ever work in construction again!

Find your why, as this is the beginning of your journey to a lucky future.

INTERNAL CONDITIONS

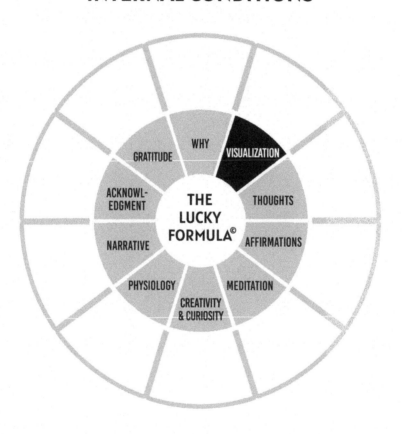

Visualization

You may remember in Part 1 when I shared my first experience regarding visualization. The day before the hockey game, I visualized how I would score three goals in one game. The visualization wasn't general but rather specific. I imagined myself scoring a certain number of times in three specific ways.

When it came time for me to play in that game, the events played out exactly how I visualized. Was it just a lucky fluke, or was it The Lucky Formula? After all, it was merely a random hockey game.

Before 2016, I might have dismissed visualization as a critical component in the formula. However, what happened that year convinced me otherwise.

In December of that year, I picked up *The Science Behind the Law of Attraction* by Dr. Srinivasan Pillay. I was searching for a mental edge and happened to find this book while researching visualization. After reading the book, I immediately put the content into practice. I wrote out, step-by-step, exactly how we would achieve the top distinction in our nutrition industry. My month-by-month plan detailed exactly what would happen and how we would blaze the trail. I gave specific numbers and situations until we achieved the goal.

I rehearsed this every single day, many times per day, starting as soon as I woke up. Early in January of 2017, I was giving a weekend seminar in Calgary, and I prepared a presentation about visualization. This presentation included my exact monthly targets from January through June. As you might guess, we hit every single target.

Again, the outsider, ignorant of the formula, might chalk up my success as a result of luck or chance, but I knew better. I was so impressed with this visualization condition that I also hired Dr. Srini to coach me personally for about a year.

Through my time with him, I learned that visualization is simply a mental rehearsal or picture you play back over and over. You create images in your mind of having something or doing something. These pictures repeat over and over again in your mind's eye, similar to an athlete visualizing scoring goals or shooting baskets. It's an incredibly powerful tool.

Visualization is simply a mental rehearsal or picture you play back over and over.

I practice visualizing by rehearsing the five steps below:

Step 1: Know what you want.

The first step to visualizing and manifesting the kind of life you want is to have a crystal-clear idea of what you want and why. There is no room for ambiguity here at all. What is your target? What is your exact goal?

Step 2: Describe your vision in great detail.

When you try to manifest the life that you want, you have to create a clear vision of what it should look like. Write this down in great detail, colors, smells, and sounds—the more granular, the better. Your brain likes details.

Step 3: Start visualizing with great emotion.

Now it's time to start envisioning the actual outcome. What emotions would you feel when achieving your ideal goal? This is also called *seeding*.

Step 4: Visualize in the first and third person.

See your goal through your own eyes. Imagine you're a boxer, throwing the punch that hits your opponent directly in the jaw. Also, take on a third-person perspective too, similar to that of a commentator.

Step 5: Take daily actions with perseverance.
For at least five minutes per day, begin imprinting your vision in your subconscious. Naturally, you will be faced with challenges and distractions. Stay focused.

These internal conditions integrate with one another. Your why flows into visualization, which in turn flows into thoughts. By tapping into these conditions, you stack the odds in your favor.

INTERNAL CONDITIONS

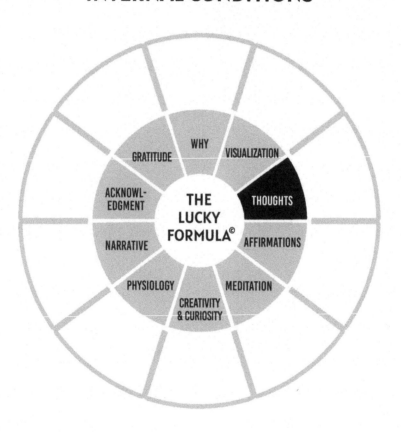

Thoughts

In some ways, humans are similar to computers. Our bodies are the hardware, and our minds are the software. Without good software, the best hardware in the world is useless. In other words, if your head is fried, your body won't work properly. Try and negotiate a deal when you're stressed or resolve a conflict between employees while you're riddled with anxiety. It's not going to happen. Your thoughts shape your results. If you are continually thinking of how difficult things are, then they will be difficult. If you constantly think that things are easy, they will be much easier. Thoughts don't simply affect us personally. They are contagious. We can feel the frequency of other people's thoughts.

> Thoughts don't simply affect us personally. They are contagious. We can feel the frequency of other people's thoughts.

Have you ever walked into a room when there is somebody who is beaming with positivity? You can absolutely feel this energy. The positivity is infectious. Think about the opposite. Have you ever been around someone plagued by fear and negativity? It's easy to feel this energy too. Some people will be turned off by these thoughts, while others will start broadcasting their own fear and negativity.

Author John Kehoe says in his book, *Mind Power*, "Weak and scattered thoughts are weak and scattered forces. Strong and concentrated thoughts are strong and concentrated forces."[4] These principles support the ancient belief that "as a person thinks in their heart, so are they." If we want specific things in our lives, we need to focus our thoughts on those things.

If you want to know someone's future reality, simply look at their present thoughts. What they think now will shape what they experience later. Kehoe goes on to teach that whatever you constantly dwell on will shape who you become. Confident thoughts create a confident person. Successful thoughts create a successful person. Loving thoughts create a loving person.

If we want to change ourselves, we must change our thoughts. Thought precedes action. If we limit our thoughts, we will, in turn, limit our future.

INTERNAL CONDITIONS

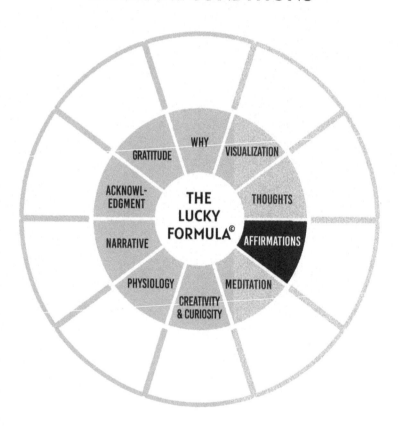

Affirmations

Affirmations are incredibly important in your journey to attract luck. They set the foundation for your day and get you focused and thinking in the right direction while building your confidence and increasing your positive vibes. According to Webster, self-affirmations are the act of "affirming one's worthiness and value as an individual for beneficial effects such as increasing one's confidence and raising self-esteem."[5]

Affirmations are often short sentences that motivate, inspire, and encourage you to take action and realize your goals. By repeating these sentences, you imprint them on your subconscious mind. This repetition can change your habits, behavior, and point of view.

Words have power. When you repeat them often, they can affect and make changes in your environment. Positive thoughts and beliefs can change your thought patterns and overcome negative self-talk.

Speak a positive future into existence.

Author John Kehoe and his book played a significant role in helping implement affirmations into my daily routine. The affirmation I first put into action was:

"I am a Fearless Leader."

I literally would tell myself this every single day for three to five minutes. I still say these affirmations today because they work. The very first week I started practicing affirmations, my life was immediately transformed! All my "little" fears started melting away.

I always remember three rules when practicing affirmations. These rules ensure that I have a positive experience.

Rule 1: Always affirm the positive.

Avoid negative thoughts like, "I am always . . ." or "I am never . . ." These statements are counterproductive and will curse your future. Who wants that? This is the exact opposite of your ideal future. Instead, use words that reflect what you want to happen. Speak a positive future into existence.

Rule 2: Make your affirmations short and simple.

Refrain from long and cumbersome phrases. Instead, use short phrases or one sentence at most. By keeping it brief, your subconscious will be able to set it on repeat automatically.

Rule 3: Don't force yourself to believe it.

Affirmations don't need opinions to work. In fact, avoid opinions altogether. Rather, just say it. You don't need to believe your affirmation; say it over and over, and it will naturally affect you.

Identify five to nine affirmations. Say your affirmations as soon as you wake up in the morning. Do a second round of affirmations for two to five minutes while you are doing your morning preparation.

For my own life, I've chosen nine affirmations I will list below.

1. I am a fearless leader.
2. I am amazing.
3. I am healthy.
4. I am abundant.
5. I am happy.
6. Life is AWESOME.
7. I am wealthy.
8. I am LUCKY.

And the last one that I recently adapted from YouTuber Jake Ducey:

9. The Miracle Working Universe comes to me and through me, guiding me in EVERYTHING that I do; EVERYTHING that I do SUCCEEDS and PROSPERS beyond my WILDEST imagination.[6]

Your affirmations can be anything that reflects a positive vibe and message. Speaking these truths out loud every single day allows you to create your new reality. The entire experience is incredibly liberating and empowering. It gets you into the right frame of mind—literally.

INTERNAL CONDITIONS

Meditation

Meditation has been the biggest game-changer in my life on every single level. It's not the mystical *woo woo* thing I thought it was fifteen years ago. It's a practice that allows the mind to feel calmer and much more focused. It has allowed me to rid my mind of demons and that little, incredibly annoying voice of anxiety or fear or negativity.

In Tim Ferris' book *Tools of Titans*, I learned about 75 to 80 percent of the hundreds of titans in his book meditate. Success leaves clues.

Meditation works, and it's experiencing widespread adoption, growing at an exponential pace due to its benefits of decreasing stress and increasing focus.

A 2015 meta-analysis on current meditation research suggests meditation as a viable treatment for conditions such as anxiety, depression, insomnia, PTSD, and burnout.[7] The case for meditation as a mental healing tool is quite convincing.

Silicon Valley elites and Wall Street gurus incorporate meditation into their lives to be more productive, balanced, and focused. Ray Dalio, the billionaire investor, has some strong views. He said, "I practice transcendental meditation, and I believe that it has enhanced my open-mindedness, higher-level perspective, equanimity, and creativity. It helps slow things down so that I can act calmly even in the face of chaos, just like a ninja in a street fight."[8]

I had a few brushes with meditation before I went all in. I started meditating when I went through bankruptcy back in 2007–2008. To calm my nerves and ease my depression, I found a type of meditation where I focused on breathing and self-exploration. The videos I discovered on YouTube were helpful for a beginner.

The second time I encountered meditation was at one of the Platinum Partners events with Tony Robbins at Sun

Valley. We had a forty-five-minute meditation session, and it opened my eyes to something I didn't recognize before. It left me with a sense of clarity—unparalleled to anything I had felt before.

I wanted that to be my norm. Done feeling stressed out of my mind, I realized I needed a better strategy.

Since then, I've gone through various meditation practices and have found some to be more effective than others. I suggest you explore the full range of meditations available. Like your body, your mind is distinct from someone else's, and you need to make sure you find the meditation style that works for you. The ones I list just happen to be the ones that worked for me.

> Like your body, your mind is distinct from someone else's, and you need to make sure you find the meditation style that works for you.

Inner Engineering is a twenty-one-minute technique developed by an Indian yogi named Sadhguru. My wife and I flew to Tampa to be trained by him directly via a two-day retreat. The technique is part breathing, part chanting, and part meditation. He had us do alternate nostril breathing and practice chants that would vibrate our bodies. We also practiced something called flutter breathing, a practice of breathing rapidly. Quick breathing prompts quicker gas exchange, in which the body's carbon dioxide levels drop while oxygen levels rise. This allows blood to carry more oxygen to the cells leading to better functioning of the body's organs and more energy. After I came out of the retreat, I definitely felt a marked difference.

The length of twenty-one minutes is perfect for my routine before going to work. I do it every morning, and if I can't for some reason, my attention is shot for the rest of the day, so I do it at night. It works for me, and that's what matters in the end. This is why in the fifty-two months since learning this technique, I have not missed one day!

Though I had great results with these techniques, that might not hold true for everyone. I tried Joe Dispenza's guided meditation, and it was great, but forty-five minutes was too long. I couldn't see myself doing it every day.

When considering meditation, choose something that fits your lifestyle. There is no point getting worked up about meditation when the whole reason for meditating is to have less anxiety.

Meditation also helped me make decisions based on facts and reality instead of on emotions. Back when I was an executive at Pivotal Payments, at times, there was in-fighting among the teams. Maybe the sales team fought against the operations team or vice versa the next week. As a sales guy, I would always take my team's side. If someone from sales came in and told me about some tiny injustice, I would literally blow up and take the salesperson's side without looking into it. Often, I would explode before having all the facts.

Meditation taught me how to take a step back, look at the facts, and then make a non-emotional decision. When you're thrown right into the moment of the conflict, you can't see clearly. Meditation allowed me to be mindful of the whole picture, not just tunnel vision.

Find a meditation method that works for you. It's simply the best way to take care of your mind. The sooner you step into it, the luckier you'll feel.

INTERNAL CONDITIONS

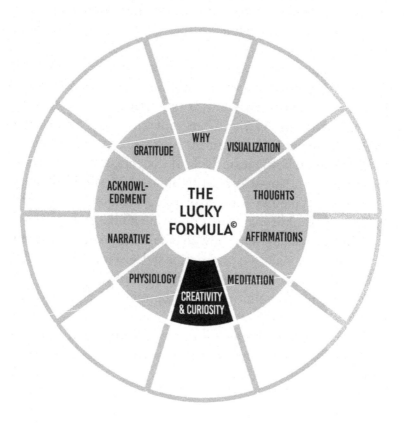

Creativity and Curiosity

Thinking outside the box requires creativity. Innovation and curiosity go hand-in-hand. Inventors, scientists, and entrepreneurs of the past and present swear by both. Notice their thoughts on curiosity:

- "I have no special talents; I am only passionately **curious**."—Albert Einstein
- "**Curiosity** keeps us moving forward, exploring, experimenting, opening new doors."—Walt Disney
- "**Curiosity** is the engine of achievement."—Ken Robinson

Now notice their insights about creativity:

- "What keeps life fascinating is the constant **creativity** of the soul."—Deepak Chopra
- "**Creativity** is intelligence having fun."—Albert Einstein
- "You can't use up **creativity**. The more you use, the more you have."—Maya Angelou

When people or organizations are both creative and curious, luck tends to visit them more often. This is why these components are part of The Lucky Formula. Think back to Part 1 when I needed to come up with $200,000. I didn't have a penny to my name, but I got creative very quickly.

And when gold no longer held its shine back in the pandemic, I got curious about investing in cryptocurrency. It paid off. A casual observer might think I got lucky, but I know the role creativity and curiosity played.

A casual observer might think I got lucky, but I know the role creativity and curiosity played.

Many companies want their employees to be more creative and curious. The truth is you can't just wish this culture into existence. Rather, it starts with the individual. You are your culture. It's a result of the way you treat other people, the way you talk to them, and how you act around them. All of this makes up your personal culture. From this space, you influence the greater culture of the group around you until it permeates throughout the entire organization.

Take, for instance, Maxy Media. I would describe our company as a setting that reflects youthful exuberance. It's a place of positivity, growth, and collaboration. People are excited to work here, and there is a general atmosphere of respect. No one is talking down to anyone else. There's no place for ego here, and everyone understands humility is the way to get things done.

We share feedback with honesty, and we take responsibility for what we've said. All of these things I have practiced from day one since opening Maxy Media. I am super aware of how I set the tone. I have tried hard to exemplify all the things that make the company culture at Maxy Media great. I know if I practiced it, the team would as well.

I have been exposed to many types of cultures, both positive and negative, constructive and toxic. One thing I know about culture is that the right one lifts everyone up. The wrong one easily destroys the morale and productivity of the group.

The best culture I have experienced is what I call a culture of growth. In this environment, we celebrate creativity and curiosity. There are no missed opportunities. Everything just clicks. Every action is maximized. The highs become even higher, and the lows become less damaging. In a culture of growth, we don't see failure as a catastrophic emergency but a challenge and a chance for learning. In my experience, a culture of growth cultivates the most luck.

INTERNAL CONDITIONS

Physiology

Physiology integrates well with creativity and curiosity. Physiology refers to the state of your body. As Tony Robbins says, "If you want to master your feelings, you must be aware of how your feelings and your body are interconnected."[9] Your body affects your feelings, and your movement dictates your feelings. The fastest way to change your feelings is to move your body. You can do this simply and without much effort.

Give this short exercise a try, and you'll see for yourself. Stand up straight. Make your spine erect and put your shoulders back. How do you feel now? Does your mindset change for the better?

When we slouch, we restrict our energy. But when we stand up straight with an erect spine, our energy is free-flowing.

We don't need to overcomplicate physiology. Sometimes the smallest tweak makes a huge difference. Here are some quick tips you can use to immediately change your physiology, which, in turn, changes your feelings.

> **We don't need to overcomplicate physiology. Sometimes the smallest tweak makes a huge difference.**

Morning

- Pop out of bed with shoulders back and eyebrows up.
- Look in the mirror for two minutes with a positive, happy, goofy smile.

Throughout the Day

- Walk with your head up and shoulders back.
- Sit with a straight spine.
- Breathe deeply.

While Meeting People

- Look straight in their eyes.
- Put your shoulders back.
- Wear a smile on your face.
- Give a strong handshake (or fist bump).

If you feel yourself getting sluggish during the day, try these tips:

- For an energy boost, start moving by taking a brisk walk.
- Consider moving your meeting outside in nature. Walk and talk.
- Get the energy flowing by playing your favorite song.

It's important to look after the small things that keep you healthy. Get enough sleep, drink plenty of water, eat smart, and keep your body moving. You'll be amazed what a difference small changes can make.

Also, consider something we often take for granted—how we smile and how often we smile. It might seem silly but smiling dramatically impacts our luck. People are more likely to engage with someone who smiles. Think about what speaking coaches tell their clients: "Pick someone in the crowd with a friendly face and make eye contact."

Smiling signals to the world that you're ready for what's next—whether it be networking, collaborating, or making a new friend. It's a gift that doesn't cost you anything except a thoughtful moment. Luck smiles upon those who smile.

INTERNAL CONDITIONS

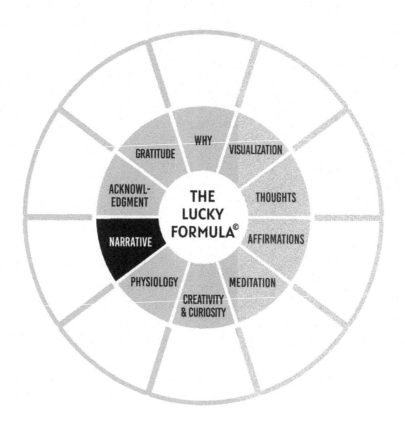

Narrative

The stories we tell ourselves shape our future. Humans live within the context of stories. My friend Kary Oberbrunner explains this in greater detail in his book, *Unhackable*.[10]

> Kids of all ages love stories. At the beginning of time, the oral tradition was how we remembered our past, understood our present, and prepared for our future.

Today, we tell stories to help us process our place in this world. We spin thousands of micro-stories every day. We'll say things like:

- You don't deserve that because . . .
- You should let someone else speak first because . . .
- Nobody values your opinion because . . .
- You aren't one of those people because . . .
- You were never good at that because . . .
- You didn't really want it anyway because . . .
- No one ever listens to you because . . .

Stories bring context and meaning to the moment. Unfortunately, these same stories often hold us back. They create prison bars around what's possible. How our stories serve us or sabotage us depends upon how we wield them.

The narrative I tell myself today creates opportunities and abundance. But at one point in my life, my stories **The narrative I tell myself today creates opportunities and abundance.** held me back from experiencing greater success and luck. Here's a peek into that period, and it centers on something called Vipassana.

I first heard about Vipassana from a woman's testimonial. She was my wife's client at the fitness business, and she suffered from major anxiety and insomnia after her parents died. She went to a ten-day Vipassana retreat, and it completely changed her life. This inspired another woman who wanted to be more positive in her life, to follow in her footsteps. That woman also came back with an incredible transformation. These two examples caught my attention, and I thought I would give it a shot as well. I was already stressed out, and I wanted to do anything to help control my emotions and inner stories.

Around 2014, when my frustration with EVO rose to its height, I went to the ten-day Vipassana retreat. It was a privately funded retreat in a small town right outside the city, and the place was supported by donations. If you couldn't afford to donate, this meant you could enjoy the stay for free.

People from all walks of life came to the retreat. I met drug addicts, people who had recently suffered a loss, alcoholics, people living with cancer, and pretty much anyone who had a story to tell.

To cultivate the peace surrounding this experience, we couldn't speak except during the meditations when we could ask questions of the leader. Until then, I had been surrounded by sound constantly as a resident in the city and part of a fast-paced business setting.

We learned about the basics of Vipassana and how it relates to controlling our stress hormones. Stress raises our cortisol levels, and the chemicals created by this increased stress stay in our bodies for a long time. When this constantly happens, the chemicals build up in the body with nowhere else to go.

This leads to unhealthiness. When confronted with stress, we're either craving something or avoiding something. If we learned to eliminate these cravings and aversions, we would feel more in control.

Every day a bell would ring to let us know it was time to go into the meditation room. For the first three days, we only practiced breathing through our noses. We would sit and breathe for ten to twelve hours a day—breathing in, breathing out. Before every meditation session, a video of S. N. Goenka, the guru who created Vipassana, would play. He explained the cravings and aversions and told us all the stress caused by our everyday lives goes to a particular spot in our body and hurts.

I agreed with his insight. My stress spot was my back. It felt tense, and it hurt. In the course of these first three days, vivid images traveled through my head. There were memories of things that had happened to me when I was a kid and memories I had completely forgotten about.

The experience invited us to cleanse our bodies by filtering out all the negative memories. One of the things I frequently saw was my mother being late. She was late to everything, while I was a punctual person. I liked being on time, and I still do, so waiting for her was one of the causes of my stress and anxiety.

The instructors also led us through an "hour of strong determination," which happened three times every day. We would pick a position, mostly sitting crossed-legged, and we couldn't move a muscle for the next hour. It was brutal.

For the first three or four nights, I couldn't sleep at all. It felt like lightning bolts firing through my body, an electrical storm in my head. I never experienced anything like it.

I learned how to focus on one thing. It was during wintertime, and I distinctly remember being so sharp. Within this surreal discipline, I would walk around the yard and count my steps. I walked all the way up to 700 steps, counting each one without missing a beat. I felt like I was wielding my attention like a sniper would, totally focused.

On the third day, we started doing a more advanced Vipassana technique, which involved moving energy around the body. First, we picked a spot on the top of our heads and concentrated on that spot until we felt it tingle. Once that happened, we did the same thing on every square inch of our bodies. At first, I calculated it took about an hour to feel that tingle everywhere.

Eventually, over the next seven days, we could push that energy through our entire bodies. For example, I felt my energy pulsing through my hand, then I focused on it to push that feeling toward my wrist, then up my arms, and beyond. The experience taught us how to be aware of our bodies and find where we had blockages—or shadows, as they called them. This was an indication that the energy was stagnant and couldn't flow. What we needed to do was to move it around. Scientifically, I think we can identify this as breaking up our cortisol or other stress chemicals stuck in our bodies.

For me, this was the most intense part of the whole retreat. I would get crazy images of things that happened to me when I was a kid. These were stressful memories buried deep in my mind.

I heard my parents yelling at me. Another time, I had a teacher reprimanding me. Or it would be my coach, shouting at me. Once again, I saw my mother being late. I saw my fellow students equally overwhelmed. Some people cried or screamed when these negative memories came back to them. I figured it was a process of cleansing all of that out of our systems.

After I came out of the Vipassana retreat, I felt like I had pushed a reset button in my head. Something got rewired in my brain, and I had an immense amount of peace and clarity. My outbursts became few and far between. I no longer woke up at three in the morning with irrational fears. I had much greater control over my emotions and focus.

The stories I told myself shifted too. My narrative was no longer negative. I replaced the shadows with light, and my stress melted away. My ability to attract luck was greatly enhanced by changing my internal voice from negative and fearful to positive and abundant.

My ability to attract luck was greatly enhanced by changing my internal voice from negative and fearful to positive and abundant.

INTERNAL CONDITIONS

Acknowledgment

You've probably heard the phrase, "Nothing succeeds like success." Luck, attraction, and success act like a magnet attracting even more luck, success, and opportunities. When you think and feel lucky, you vibrate with that kind of amazing energy.

Sometimes we have difficulty getting into that lucky energy state. The internal condition of acknowledgment helps you get there.

Acknowledgment reflects on your life and identifies major wins you have had in your past. Everybody has events and circumstances they felt good about—things they did well.

People who are already successful and lucky attract even greater luck because of the nature of their predominant thoughts. The luck vibration is a great asset to possess and broadcast. If you do not have this vibration, don't worry. The acknowledgment technique will help you get there.

> **People who are already successful and lucky attract even greater luck because of the nature of their predominant thoughts.**

The technique is simple. Make a list of twenty amazing things you have done in your past:

- Are you a great father?
- Are you a great mother?
- Are you an incredible friend?
- Are you positive?
- Are you generous?
- Are you a great athlete?
- Did you ace an exam?
- Did you win a race, a spelling bee, or a jiu-jitsu tournament?

You are not limited to somebody else's definition of success. There is no need to be rich, famous, or gorgeous-looking. There are hundreds of things to look at in your life.

After learning about this technique, I created my list of twenty. I was blown away at the list and felt truly amazing about what I had accomplished. Here is the actual list that I created:

1. I have two amazing boys and a beautiful wife and family.
2. I have incredible friends.
3. I have five businesses that produce recurring revenue.
4. I own one of the biggest TikTok Advertising agencies in the world.
5. We have over 100 incredible staff members.
6. I wrote a practical and helpful book called *The Lucky Formula*.
7. I am a best-selling author.
8. I have the greatest formula that will change the world.
9. I was a sports agent and enjoyed the perks of hanging with professional athletes.
10. I have successfully exited four companies.
11. Both of my brothers played professional hockey.
12. We are the number one distributor of health products in Canada for the largest nutrition company in the world.
13. I have a strong circle of influence.
14. I am healthy and eat incredibly well.
15. I have a personal chef.
16. I meditate every single day.
17. I do personal development every single day.
18. I am wealthy.

19. I just earned my blue belt in jiu-jitsu.
20. I train five times per week.

Take the time *right now* to do your acknowledgment list of twenty phenomenal things and see how you feel after. If you are ever feeling down, simply look at this list, and you'll feel incredible and lucky again.

INTERNAL CONDITIONS

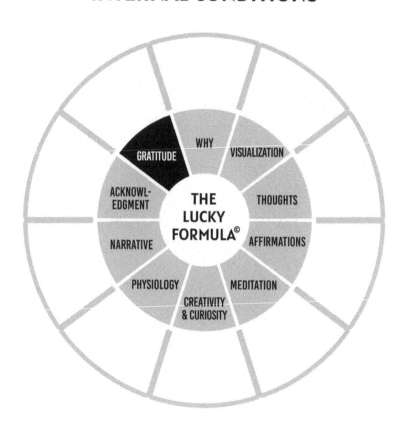

Gratitude

We all have a choice about what we focus on. Some people take account of everything they *don't* have. This habit cultivates an attitude of jealousy and ungratefulness, leading to scarcity and lack.

Lucky people do the opposite. They take account of everything they *do* have. As a result, they experience gratitude, leading to resourcefulness and abundance.

Peter Diamandis, the founder and chairman of the XPRIZE Foundation, has a great perspective about gratitude. He says in our present day, each of us has the privilege to work on the world's most critical problems. In previous generations, this was only possible for governments and wealthy philanthropists. Essentially, problem-solving has become democratized. Today we can all participate in it, and therefore we should all be grateful for that fact.

I had never thought of problem-solving from that perspective, but he is right. We have the ability right now to change the world just through an internet connection and a laptop. How crazy is that? Moreover, how amazing is it that we live in a time that allows this to happen?

Diamandis' point is exactly this: A mindset of gratitude always shifts perspectives and expectations to that of thankfulness. It flips moments of negativity into opportunity.

> **A mindset of gratitude always shifts perspectives and expectations to that of thankfulness.**

This is important for a few reasons:

1. **Gratitude allows self-reflection**: A mindset of gratitude allows you to appreciate every aspect of any situation properly.

2. **Gratitude allows for learning moments**: In times of failure, a mindset of gratitude gives you the readiness to learn from your faults. I no longer look back on my failed real estate venture as a stain on my business history. Instead, I see it as a valuable lesson in business and relationships. I learned so much, but I don't make those mistakes anymore. I am certainly grateful for that.

3. **Gratitude rallies people, including yourself**: Gratitude is a concept that sees infinite possibilities. In a thankless mindset, there is give and take. There is win and lose. There is you versus me. Ungrateful people only think about themselves. If they don't have it, it means somebody else does. People like this crumble inward during times of crisis, with barely anyone to help them. Grateful people, however, keep going because they know there is always an upside. Moreover, gratitude connects people and allows them to win as one. A mindset of gratitude pulls everyone like gravity.

4. **Gratitude can help you spot opportunities**: Let's say a big failure happens. If you are a grateful person, you turn this around and spot the opportunity. This is exactly what happened when Maxy Media lost its main business through our Facebook ban. We suddenly found ourselves in a moment where our company was essentially lost. But we didn't back down. We saw this as an opportunity to venture elsewhere, to grab ahold of another market. So we did, and as of this moment, we are a leading TikTok advertising agency in North America.

Cultivate gratitude everywhere in your life, especially if you experience negative events. Life is all about making the most of every moment, and a grateful mindset enables you to do just that. Life doesn't start or stop with us. We're all connected and interdependent, and we have the opportunity to cultivate generosity, resourcefulness, and abundance.

A very simple technique that I learned from Dan Sullivan was to focus on your three wins of the day. He created a downloadable app called WinStreak.® At the end of every day, I open the app and log my three wins of the day. This is an incredibly empowering way to go to sleep and show your gratitude. The people who embody gratitude are the luckiest indeed.

☘ ☘ ☘

These ten internal conditions integrate well with one another. Skip one condition and you'll decrease your chance at luck. Take narrative, for example. You can perfect the other nine conditions, but if you continually tell yourself negative stories, you won't have a positive outlook and feel good about yourself much less stay lucky. The same can be said about visualization. If you never visualize a positive outcome, it's likely you won't experience one. All ten conditions must be leveraged if you want to cash in on success.

EXTERNAL CONDITIONS

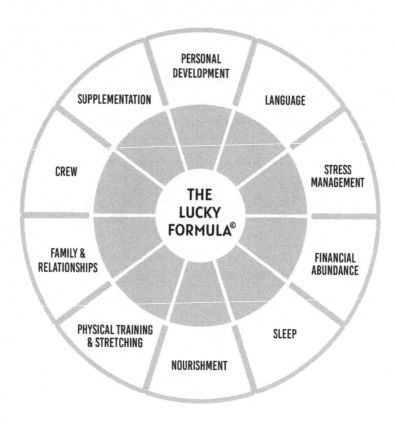

9

External Conditions

Your outside world is a reflection of your inside world.
What goes on in the inside shows on the outside.
—Bob Proctor

In the previous chapter, we discovered how success is an internal job. While this is true, success always shows up externally too. Our external experience is closely linked with our internal reality.

As a result, The Lucky Formula diagram reveals ten external components as well. We'll unpack them one at a time.

EXTERNAL CONDITIONS

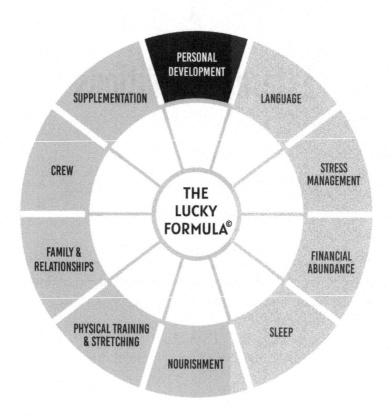

Personal Development

If you want to be lucky, engaging in personal development daily is a must. Personal development is a set of activities that expands your capabilities and potential. It enhances your quality of life and helps you realize your dreams and goals. Getting better every day is a necessity if you want to attract luck.

Personal development is a never-ending process that you will do until your final day. It can include reading books, watching videos, and listening to podcasts or audiobooks. It could involve attending workshops and seminars that sharpen your skills.

A great example of personal development from my life is when I participated in Dan Sullivan's Strategic Coach® quarterly workshops. I am always blown away at the simplicity of his philosophy and how effective these strategies have been for my life and in business.

When I walked into the room where our first workshop was hosted, Dan wrote the word "STUFF" on the board. My first impulse was, "I spent all this money to learn about the word *stuff*?!"

Believe it or not, that word has had the single biggest impact on my skill to attract luck and expand business. The key point is to do only what is important and pertains to you. Get rid of all distracting emails, text messages, and phone calls, and free yourself of everything that's not your Unique Ability®, in a word—*stuff*!

The second biggest impact that these seminars gave me was viable contacts: millionaires, billionaires, movers, and shakers. Kary Oberbrunner, my publisher, is a global

Get rid of all distracting emails, text messages, and phone calls, and free yourself of everything that's not your Unique Ability®, in a word—*stuff*!

influencer in the industry. If it were not for Dan's group, I never would have met him.

A powerful tip for remembering and embodying the material you are learning is to simultaneously read a book and listen to the audio. When you read the physical book and listen to the audiobook while driving or exercising, this makes the content stick.

I encourage everyone to start their personal development journey by reading *Think and Grow Rich* by Napoleon Hill. This is the first book my father gave me. In my view, this is the foundation of all other personal development books. Many of the techniques that Mr. Hill discusses are mentioned in *The Lucky Formula* as well. These topics include how to create a burning desire, how to develop faith, and how to visualize.

Mr. Hill constantly repeats the fact that thoughts and a burning desire are powerful things. Thinking is more conducive to success than anything else. He reiterates time and again that the person who *thinks* the right thoughts with a burning desire and persistence will absolutely succeed.

Influencers in this space often say, "Leaders are readers." I add my own spin and say, "Lucky leaders are readers." For this reason, in the appendix, I have provided you with a list of recommended books that I suggest reading or listening to. If you choose to do so, it will increase your chances of getting lucky.

EXTERNAL CONDITIONS

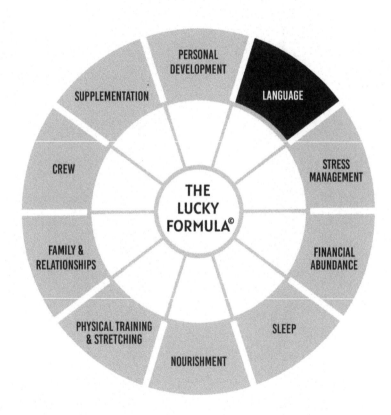

Language

The way we speak to other people matters. I have a friend who says, "Words create worlds." It's true. Words are so powerful; they shape the level of luck we experience. Certain words attract people, and certain words repel others. The language we use can heal or kill, especially when we're in a position of authority.

I have employees who have left Maxy Media and told me I was the best boss they had ever worked for. I believe it has something to do with the language I used. I like the reputation I have cultivated, but it's only a side effect.

Using positive words and phrases tends to produce higher levels of engagement than negative words and phrases.

Using positive words and phrases tends to produce higher levels of engagement than negative words and phrases.

Try Saying These Words

- Thank you.
- I appreciate it.
- Awesome.
- Brilliant!
- Glad to have you here.

All of these words will add way more value than negative expressions.

After observing an impressive feat, a leader might say something like, "Nice job."

Lucky leaders take it a step further. Add to the compliment. Say something like, "Nice job . . . and I really appreciate your attention to delivering a high level of quality on this project."

Don't be afraid to insert body language too. It's powerful. A thumbs up, a smile, or a high-five goes a long way to provide encouragement and positive reinforcement.

The external condition of language flows from the internal conditions of thoughts and narrative. If we are serious about personal development, then that work will show up in our words.

This is not a new concept. Rather, it's an ancient principle. Notice this saying from the first century: "By their fruit you will recognize them. Are grapes gathered from thornbushes, or figs from thistles? Likewise, every good tree bears good fruit, but a bad tree bears bad fruit. A good tree cannot bear bad fruit, and a bad tree cannot bear good fruit."

What "fruit" is your language producing—healthy fruit or unhealthy fruit? That choice is up to you. There's nothing lucky about it.

EXTERNAL CONDITIONS

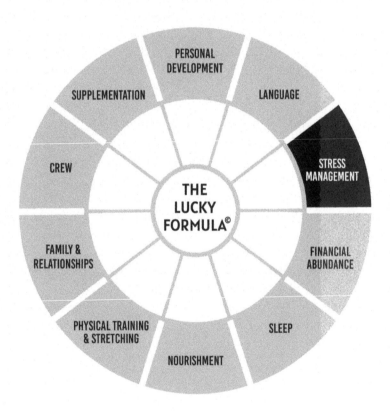

Stress Management

I used to be a very emotional and sometimes volatile guy, launching into outbursts for reasons that should not have concerned me. I had a sales executive who would come into my office and always beg for money or advances. I screamed at him to get him out of my office because he got on my nerves so much. More than once, my tirade would leave me feeling run down for a day or two.

I'm no stranger to stress and pressure. When growth is on the line, the pace is fast, and speed always takes a toll on the mind. Coupled with the ever-present threat of survival, things can always go south, even when they seem great.

I've been in situations where cash flow was positive right out of the gate, such as Maxy Media. In such cases, there is much less stress because at least we can make payroll. Then there are times when money is constantly a problem. This was the situation at EVO Payments in the beginning. The company stayed in the red for about two years while it grew to 150 employees. After about two years of hard work, we finally got in the black, and the company was highly profitable.

I would often wake up at three in the morning in the middle of the night with crazy thoughts running through my head. Is the board going to fire me? Will I be replaced as CEO? Being a nervous wreck like this didn't help me at all, and I was stressed out of my mind—constantly overwhelmed by work.

A calm mind increases your chances of luck. A cluttered mind misses even the most obvious opportunities. When you're stressed, you often prolong your misfortunes. Back when I was in that real estate investment hell, I should have

> **A calm mind increases your chances of luck. A cluttered mind misses even the most obvious opportunities.**

had the foresight to cut my losses early and move on. But I didn't.

And back when I ran EVO, I used to be cc'd on every email. No matter how small it was, I had to know about it. A sale just happened? I had to know about it. A minor HR issue arose? I had to know about it. How else would I make the important decisions if I didn't?

This was where I was dead wrong. This kind of mindset wasn't helpful. In fact, all it was doing was harming me and my productivity because I was paying attention to too many things that weren't contributing much to the bottom line.

I was a victim of what I call the Entrepreneur's Dilemma—when you feel you have to be the best at everything. I had to be the one who knew the most about marketing, operations, sales, accounting, and anything else. As you can imagine, this didn't end well.

It wasn't until I sought out business coaching with Tony Robbins and Dan Sullivan that I realized this was the wrong way to think. I needed to learn how to delegate to relieve that stress. Trusting my people would have empowered them to be better at their jobs, which would have improved the company's operations at the same time.

Some managers make the mistake of thinking managing an employee means micromanaging them. Such managers are paranoid to no end. This is no way to foster respect and build trust. It's important to trust others, especially if you're working together. It goes for partnerships too. No one wants to work with a nagging business partner who constantly checks to see if you are holding up your side of the bargain.

If you want to build something big, you have to relinquish control and allow others to shine. I've discovered that delegating is easier when you follow these four simple steps:

1. **Ensure you have the right person in the first place**: If you don't have the right people to delegate to, chances are you are in for a nasty surprise.

2. **Communicate clear goals and expectations**: Be clear about what you want others to achieve when you delegate. Tell them what "a job well done" looks like and when you want it done. The more details, the better.

3. **Track progress with feedback**: Delegating does not mean throwing a task at someone and just letting them do whatever they want. Make sure to check in now and then to see if they're doing good work. Delegating means trust, but it also means making sure others feel you still have their back. Give as much feedback as possible, so they know what you envision as the end goal. Delegating is a conversation.

4. **Give greater purpose**: When you delegate, make sure they feel part of the bigger picture. They need to know what they are fighting for. At Maxy Media, I reiterate that our goal is to become the number one social media advertising company in the world. That is a goal everyone can rally behind.

According to Dan Sullivan, delegating properly is a skill that will give your team new possibilities and reduce your stress once put into place correctly.

Even more than that, it will free you. You will be liberated to do things you want to do, the things that give you incredible energy, the things that push the needle, and these things always eliminate your stress.

EXTERNAL CONDITIONS

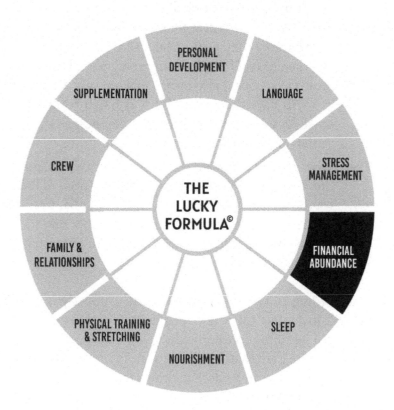

Financial Abundance

Financial stress is the worst type of stress. When the need for money dominates your thoughts, it severely inhibits your ability to generate luck. In the area of finances, I've made it a point to learn from people smarter than me. In one of Tony Robbins' masterminds, I met incredible financial influencers, such as T. Boone Pickens, the billionaire oil tycoon from Texas, and Eric Sprott from Toronto, also a billionaire. I learned quite a bit from Mr. Pickens. He talked about having a financial fortress built around oneself and how that shields us from risk. I still follow that principle today.

> **When the need for money dominates your thoughts, it severely inhibits your ability to generate luck.**

He taught us how to buy oil futures, then hedge that bet. Long story short, right after that session, I turned around, called my broker, did exactly as he told us to do, and overnight I made $30,000. It was the quickest $30,000 I had ever made. Mr. Sprott spoke about physical silver and gold and how they can help you hedge against disaster. Around that time, I started buying silver and gold assets, which proved a lifesaver during market downturns.

The majority of adults are deep in debt. Financial abundance and bad debt don't mix. Bad debt is any debt not associated with generating revenue. Credit card debt, high-interest loans, and high financing charges are all examples of bad debt. On the other hand, examples of good debt are mortgages on rental properties and lines of credit used for revenue-generating investments.

Two books that focused me on my path to financial success are *The Automatic Millionaire* by David Bach and *The Richest Man in Babylon* by George S. Clason.

Both of these powerful books have a similar message. Both were instrumental in getting me out of debt and onto solid financial footing. Here are a few of my favorite takeaways:

1. Pay yourself first automatically.

   o Invest 10 to 20 percent of your salary into a separate savings account.
   o Keep this money separate from your main account.
   o You will naturally adjust to the standard of living.
   o Deposit your paycheck into this separate account automatically.
   o Set up a direct deposit, so you never see your paycheck.

2. Fund your "rainy day" emergency account automatically.

   o Having an emergency fund is essential. What happens if you lose your job? What happens if something breaks in your house?
   o Make sure to transfer your cash over automatically to your emergency account.
   o Set aside three months of living expenses in another separate account.

3. Bach's trademarked idea for building wealth is what he calls The Latte Factor®.

   o Consider how much it costs for a latte at Starbucks. Do you truly need it?
   o Cut out unnecessary expenses with a list of must-haves.

4. Pay your credit card bills automatically.

   o   Get out of debt! After destroying your debt, make sure to pay off your credit card every month.

   o   Interest is a waste of money!

5. Pay all your monthly bills automatically.

   o   Schedule all of your utility and monthly bills automatically, so you don't forget.

After being rid of debt, the lucky leader will next look at recurring revenue businesses or investments. These types of investments have been my secret weapon to sleeping well and attracting more luck.

Obviously, this is not a financial advice book. However, I will suggest a few ideas on how to generate passive recurring income.

- Dividend-paying stocks; 2 to 5 percent dividend payouts
- Payment processing portfolios
- Real estate: rental revenue
- Direct sales businesses: These present an awesome opportunity for recurring revenue.
- Owning Amazon and Wal-Mart ecommerce stores
- Performance marketing
- Cryptocurrency stacking and lending

I unpack these concepts in greater detail in The Lucky Formula course. However, this gives you a great starting point.

As you might imagine, similar to the internal conditions, the external conditions also integrate with one another.

Notice how the condition of financial abundance integrates well with the concepts of *crew*, *nourishment and supplementation*, and *sleep*. If you don't have financial resources, you can't hire the right people (crew), purchase healthy food (nourishment and supplementation), or devote the proper time for rest (sleep).

This is what makes The Lucky Formula so powerful—the integration of the internal and external conditions.

EXTERNAL CONDITIONS

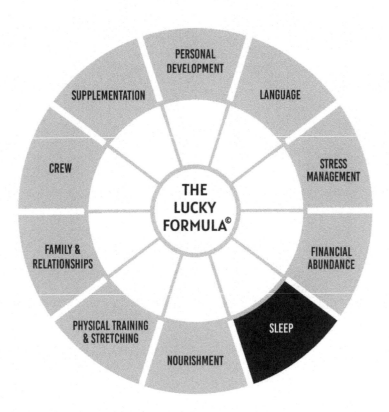

Sleep

The body is designed to literally heal itself through sleep. Skip a night of rest, and you're destroying your chance of getting lucky—literally. When you don't sleep, you simply can't perform at optimum levels. There were times in my life when I had a horrible time sleeping. This greatly affected how my mind operated and the results I therefore generated.

Men need an average of six to eight hours of sleep a night, and women need an average of seven to eight hours. Research reveals women need slightly more sleep than men due to physical and psychological differences.[11]

In my own journey, I've discovered seven tips for increasing sleep.

1. **Go to bed before your second wind**. Your body naturally gets tired. Although it might be tempting to cram in more activity, it's wiser to listen to your body. If you don't go to sleep during that period, you will get a cortisol-driven second wind that can keep you awake until the middle of the night. Rather than fighting sleep, welcome it.

2. **Choose the right type of light**. After 9:00 p.m., use red light instead of blue light and avoid white light. Even five minutes of blue light from a computer or smart phone screen shuts off your melatonin production for four hours. Blue light also suppresses melatonin. In fact, light of any kind suppresses the secretion of melatonin. This sabotages the quality of your sleep as confirmed by research from the Cleveland Clinic.[12] Ideally, avoid screens in the evening entirely. Regarding your cell phone, change the screen to red light. A simple google search of "red light background on IOS" will offer a

solution. For at least an hour before going to bed, try to avoid bright lights.

3. **Fill up with fat at dinner.** Rather than experiencing carb crashes, sugar rushes, and caffeine fixes, choose healthy fats. This is because fat is a long-burning fuel for your mind and body. The shorter fats of MCT oil are converted into ketones and immediately used as fuel for your brain. MCT oil also helps you burn body fat while you sleep.

4. **Consume protein.** Muscle repair occurs at night during deep sleep. Our bodies use protein for muscle repair and immune function. Choosing the right proteins ensures your body has all the raw materials it needs to heal and grow new tissue.

   Muscle repair occurs at night during deep sleep. Our bodies use protein for muscle repair and immune function.

5. **Don't drink coffee in the evening.** Similar to exercising too close to bedtime, drinking coffee too close to bedtime is unwise as well. Coffee stimulates your mind and can increase productivity. However, you need to let your mind rest after its high-output performances.

6. **Decrease your stress.** Perhaps the most common reason people report not being able to sleep is that they don't know how to clear their minds and stop worrying. Deep breathing exercises can do wonders for helping your brain shut down. Avoid troublesome news, email inboxes, and mindless scrolling right before bed.

7. **Don't exercise near bedtime.** Exercise is a great thing, but you can do it at the wrong time. Exercise raises your cortisol levels, which interferes with sleep. You should not exercise for at least two hours before going to bed

unless you count restorative yoga and breath training as exercise.

Sleep is critical to getting lucky. If you're too tired, you'll miss hearing opportunity knocking. Your beauty sleep can also be called your lucky sleep!

EXTERNAL CONDITIONS

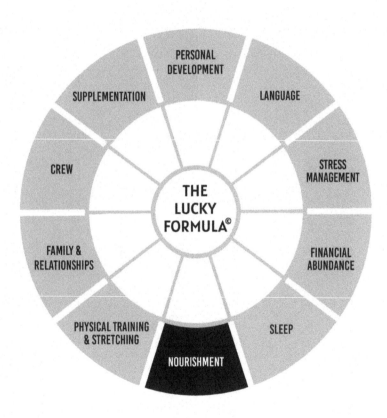

Nourishment

Regarding implementing new ways of eating into your daily routine, I believe you should try something at least one time. If it doesn't work, eliminate it.

When I tried intermittent fasting, there seemed to be some evidence behind it. I read how it dropped insulin levels, facilitated fat burning, and increased muscle gain. The benefits seemed worthy enough for me to try it out. Not long after, I realized it made me dizzy. I couldn't work because I couldn't focus. As a result, I stopped immediately.

It might have been working its magic behind the scenes, reconfiguring my body's hormone levels, but I couldn't stand it long enough to find out. It didn't work for me, and I'll probably never try it again.

Many years ago, my wife and I used to eat at her family's house three to four days a week. I can remember going there and eating whatever they served. Home-cooked meals never go wrong. Then after the meal, I would have these thick Dutch cookies, which would have a slather of chocolate on each. They were amazing. I would eat around five of them each time I visited. On top of that, I would drink two glasses of wine, which is normal for a typical European dinner.

At the time, I was playing hockey three days a week, and I was an active guy. I used to work outside, and I grew up playing sports all the time. Naturally, I assumed I was in shape. After hockey, I'd go to the pub, drink beer with the team, and eat junk food like chicken wings and fries.

Then reality finally hit me. I realized I needed to take better care of my body, so I made drastic changes. Today I feel fantastic, far better than I did twenty-five years ago.

Health is where everything starts. Your body is your hardware, and you have to maintain its optimal state. All our bodies have the potential to perform like luxury cars. But unless you care for it like you would a Ferrari, you will not get much out of it. In fact, it's going to break down, and you will feel much worse than a beat-up junker.

Health is where everything starts. Your body is your hardware, and you have to maintain its optimal state.

This book is obviously not a book about health and nutrition, and I'm in no way qualified to give anyone a professional opinion about what you should eat and what exercises you should do, but I have provided you with some superfoods that will increase your energy levels.

THE LUCKY FORMULA

FOODS FOR BRAIN POWER

Computer programmers are fond of using the acronym GIGO when a poorly written program fails. Garbage In, Garbage Out. The same is true of our bodies. If we eat food low in nutritional value (garbage in), our bodies and our minds don't function well (garbage out). What if we were to rework that acronym. Good In, Good Out. Good food in, good results out. The following foods are key components of my diet. When I regularly include them in my meals, I have higher levels of energy for longer periods of time and my thinking is clearer.

FATTY FISH	NUTS & SEEDS	BERRIES	WHOLE GRAINS
Salmon	Flaxseed	Avocado	Barley
Mackerel	Hemp hearts	Black currants	Brown rice
Tuna	Pumpkin seeds	Blackberries	Oatmeal
Sardines	Sunflower seeds	Blueberries	
	Almonds	Mulberries	
	Cashews	Strawberries	
	Hazelnuts		
	Peanuts		

CRUCIFEROUS VEGETABLES	GREEN LEAFY VEGETABLES	OTHER	BEVERAGES
Broccoli	Kale	Eggs	Coffee
Cabbage	Spinach	Dark Chocolate	Green Tea
Cauliflower			
Turnips			

In terms of food, I try to eat at least every three hours or so to get my metabolism going. I'll typically start the morning off with a meal replacement shake because it takes less time and I need to get to the office quickly. When I get into my office, I don't eat right away. I'll spread almond butter on gluten-free sprouted bread. Then I'll have another shake a little after that.

As for lunch, which for me is around 1:00 to 2:00 p.m., I like to have a three-egg omelet with spinach, peppers, and mushrooms. Sometimes I'll add some smoked salmon. For dinner, I usually incorporate salads, proteins, and some carbohydrates. I'll also change this around every now and then to see what works better.

Here is a suggested menu for a typical day:

Breakfast:
1 cup Greek yogurt with ½ cup berries OR
2-egg omelet with spinach or other vegetables

Lunch:
Bean and vegetable soup OR
2 cups vegetables with fish (salmon or tuna, for example)

Dinner:
Salad with chicken or turkey
(Salad base: lettuce, peppers, cucumbers, celery, and cabbage)

The way you approach nutrition matters. Too many people dive into it without thinking and then burn out from their program and resort back to bad habits. The key is to do something sustainable. The goal is a healthy lifestyle, not just a healthy lunch.

EXTERNAL CONDITIONS

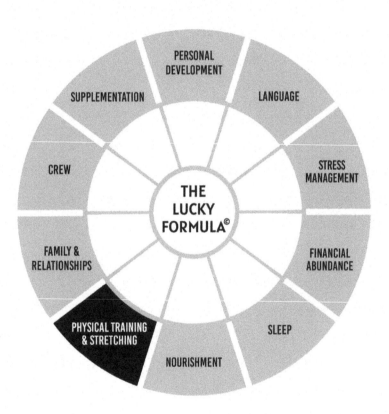

Physical Training and Stretching

When I first got focused on my health and fitness, I was at 23 percent body fat and not feeling good at all. With a great nutrition and training regimen, I was able to get down to below 8 percent body fat, and I weighed just 164 pounds. I was shredded, but it was completely unsustainable. I'm a busy guy and trying to maintain that body consumed me so much I couldn't pay attention to other things in my life.

Maintaining a body that's healthy, active, and free of chronic pain is something most people desire. You look better, you stand up straighter, you feel more confident, and you have more energy to take on the day.

Exercise increases your overall health and sense of well-being, but it also integrates direct stress-busting benefits. Physical activity bumps up the production of your brain's feel-good neurotransmitters—endorphins. Although this function is often referred to as a runner's high, any aerobic activity, such as a rousing game of tennis or a hike in nature, produces the same effects.

> Exercise increases your overall health and sense of well-being, but it also integrates direct stress-busting benefits.

Physical training reduces the negative effects of stress and improves your cardiovascular, digestive, and immune systems. This, in turn, protects your body. I call it "meditation in motion." After a fast-paced game of racquetball, a long walk, or several laps in the pool, you may often find you've forgotten the day's irritations. As you shed your daily tensions through movement and physical activity, you may find the resulting energy and optimism helps you stay calm, clear, and focused on everything you do.

Exercise improves your mood, lowering depression and anxiety. It can also improve your sleep, which stress often disrupts. You'll feel more confident and in control over your body and your life.

EXTERNAL CONDITIONS

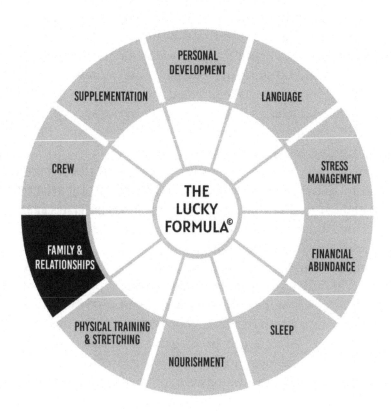

Family and Relationships

I'm a natural cheerleader, and I try to uplift people's morale all the time. Of course, some people think I'm putting up a facade, but I'm not. I'm genuinely happy most of the time, and I want people around me to be that way.

Maybe I got it from my mother. I often think of her as "happy-go-lucky." My brothers and I agree we are very fortunate to be her sons. She was a vibrant soul, one who literally lit up the room whenever she entered. Even right before her last breath, she was quick with a joke: "I am ready to go, but I ain't going," with her trademark smirk. Family matters, and my mother mattered to me. I will always remember how much she backed us up and supported us no matter what.

One time I was giving a friend named Alex a ride in my car, and he asked me, "Mark, why are you so positive and pumped all the time?"

Instead of giving him an answer, I asked him how his work was going. He gave me a boring response. I pulled the car over and stared straight into his eyes and showered him with enthusiastic compliments. I told him, with all the sincerity inside me:

"Alex, you're doing an amazing job!"

"You are a total champion, a complete rockstar!"

"Alex, you are the best in the world at what you do!"

Then I asked him, "How do you feel now?"

He told me he felt great about his work, and that was despite the fact that he knew exactly what I was doing; I had injected positive energy into him and his work, and it made him feel amazing.

That's what positivity does. It's a tangible energy that injects life into people. People respond better to positivity. Negativity has never lifted anyone up in human history. Positivity contributes to more success in the workplace. People with a positive perspective will achieve higher incomes in general.

People with a positive perspective will achieve higher incomes in general.

Positivity in relationships, be it with family or friends, is a force that drives something forward, not backward. It pushes you instead of holding you back. Positivity gives you the expectation of a better tomorrow.

If you are a negative person and you expect bad things to happen in your life, when good things occur, you're more likely to brush it off as an accident that's outside of your control. If you take the perspective of positivity, you flip this around. You expect good things to happen, and you will interpret bad things as outside of your control.

Moreover, family and friends want to be around positive people. If someone constantly complains about how he does not make enough money, how he hates his job, and how he can't get a girlfriend, this repels luck.

Think about a completely different person. Imagine another guy talking about how he is working toward making more money soon, improving at his job, finding love one day, and in the meantime enjoying being single. They're both going through the same situation, but it sounds completely different. Which guy would you want to hang out with?

As a father and husband, I make it a point to speak words of life to my family. I often tell friends that I might believe in them too much. Of course, I'm being sarcastic. But the truth is I tell them they can do anything. I pump them up with so much positivity that they ooze confidence. I'd rather my family be full of belief than empty of hope. The world tries to grind us down enough with negative messages. It's refreshing to give those you love the gift of belief.

Nothing brings more luck than positive, healthy relationships. People bring ideas, opportunities, and good fortune. The fact you have a mindset that attracts people to you means you're setting yourself up to be luckier.

None of us knows how long we have with the people in our lives. This is why I try to make the most of every relationship, whether my family or my colleagues. People notice when you're intentional and authentic. Here's an email I once received from an employee who used to work for me at Maxy Media.

Hi, Mark,

I just wanted to say thanks for having me at Maxy Media and for giving me an opportunity to contribute. It was an excellent learning experience. One of the things I learned from you was how you were always on the ball and never panicked. I am inspired by the stability you showed during the tougher times, even when everyone else was going crazy, the way you held your guard, and the vision you had that the crisis was temporary and that the company would get through it pretty soon.

You are truly a great leader, and I never felt like the office was dull or not lively enough, as you were always there to cheer everyone up with your ecstatic demeanor.

I regret we didn't get a chance to go on a second mission, but I appreciate you thinking highly of me. I wish I had taken a few more chances to bounce off ideas with you and have a conversation to get insights from your entrepreneurial adventures.

I wish you and the company continued success, and I hope I get a chance to work with you someday.

I would certainly work with him again in a heartbeat if the opportunity arose. The point is, people remember positive people, especially a leader. Energy goes from top to bottom.

It may be an obvious point, but positivity is something many people often forget. Of course, it's easy to lose sight of hoping for a better tomorrow when you're in a crisis. If anyone knows about that, it's me. But I encourage you to keep smiling. It's a hell of a lot better than bringing down everyone else, including yourself.

Very few people take an inventory of their relationships. At the end of the day, if you don't know how people influence you, you won't know who to keep close to or who to distance yourself from.

Think about how certain people affect your life. Do you have a person who causes negative emotions to arise within you? Do you know someone who constantly throws doubt into your life without offering any valid reason for it? You need to weed out these people. This is tough work because many times these toxic people can be your friends or even family. But if they drag you down, is it truly worth holding on to these relationships? Be brutally honest about who deserves a spot at your table.

On the other hand, do you have someone in your life who constantly steps up to help you out? Are there people who always seem to be coming up with ways to solve your problems? These are the people you want to invest in. They are in harmony with your life's goals.

The more you take inventory of how people affect you, the better you'll be able to identify who can give you what you need to succeed. Start establishing the right circle of influence around you and leave out those who don't serve your goals.

External Conditions

No matter how talented you are, you cannot be truly successful without people. Getting lucky is often a group effort. I can't imagine enjoying all the lucky breaks I've experienced without the people who helped me get there.

EXTERNAL CONDITIONS

Crew

As the leader of a fitness and nutrition business for years, I know the normal pattern people go through when they get serious about training and eating. They'll show up for the first few sessions, pumped up and ready to go. They'll work out, feel motivated, and start making progress. But soon after, the initial burst of energy will dwindle. There will be more excuses to skip, and eventually, exercise will become a fading memory.

Tony Robbins said, "Without accountability, you'll always blame your circumstances on forces beyond your control. If you have trouble holding yourself accountable, consider working with a [coach] who can push you to reach your full potential."[13]

He's right. Personal accountability is tough. You need a crew in work, life, health, and every other area.

It's always better to share the load. Motivation is like carrying a weight. Many days you will feel like you can take it all on your own, but there will be days when all you want to do is drop it on the ground. That's why someone else is there to carry it with you and—at times—for you.

I knew this would also happen with me, so right away, I found a trainer who would keep me coming to the gym regularly. If I felt that my motivation was waning, I could depend on my trainer to proverbially kick my butt and get me training that day.

When I went full-time into the fitness business, I would hold group workout classes for my clients. These were effective in bringing people back again and again. In this way, everyone could use each other as accountability partners. Whenever someone didn't show up, we would ask where that person was. This type of group dynamic kept people on their toes and created a positive feedback loop on one another.

There are many ways to do this. Just getting a friend to go work out with you could get the job done. Anything that can remind you that you need to get up and get going will work.

Choosing your crew transcends workouts in the gym. Your crew goes with you, wherever you go. One such place could be a mastermind.

> **Your crew goes with you, wherever you go. One such place could be a mastermind.**

I first heard about the mastermind concept by reading Napoleon Hill. He came up with the idea after studying notable legends in business, including Henry Ford, John D. Rockefeller, and Thomas Edison. There have been many interpretations of what a mastermind is, but the definition I like most is Napoleon Hill's. In his book, *Think and Grow Rich*, he says the core principle of a mastermind is "the coordination of knowledge and effort of two or more people, who work toward a definite purpose, in the spirit of harmony."[14]

This is exactly what's happening when you see amazing companies rise up from seemingly nowhere. And it's why some leaders seem larger than life. They're not superhuman. Rather, they're tapping into a source greater than any one person. Hill continues, "No two minds ever come together without thereby creating a third, invisible, intangible force, which may be likened to a third mind [the mastermind]."

I've benefitted from participating in masterminds throughout my career. They've taken me further, faster. I'm so committed to the concept that I started The Lucky Formula Mastermind©. This group of high performers attracts some of the most successful people on the planet. People love it because it provides a practical space to work out the Lucky Formula in real time.

When assembling your crew, there are four important things you need to take into account.

First, you need to know where you're going. Without a destination, you have no purpose. A team without a purpose is only a group of people talking in circles.

All great people who had amazing teams push them to success knew where they were going. Elon Musk's destination was to launch reusable rockets into space and make electric cars. Jeff Bezos' destination was to create a store that would sell everything through the web.

In both cases, they had a clear North Star that enabled them to know what kind of knowledge they needed around them. Once you know what knowledge you need, the rest is simple. You only need to go out and find the people with that knowledge.

Second, you need to know what your needs are. There is nothing worse to a team than someone who has no role to play because that's just dead weight. A team is like an engine. If you're not constantly running it, you're letting it get rusty, and if you're staying still while running it, you're wasting energy.

Third, you need to relinquish control. A good team allows different people to take up the space they know best, and for that, you need to give up space. Thus, it is important to establish your goals before organizing the right team. What is your team for? What do you want to achieve with your team? This will guide how you assemble your crew and prevent you from wasting time and energy.

Fourth, you have to check your ego. When you organize a crew, you must surround yourself with people smarter than you, and you can't do that unless you drop your ego.

It is said that Mark Zuckerberg would not make the cut if he tried to get a job as a developer these days, not even in his own company. He does not need to code. That is not his concern. Thus, he does not know the most about coding in his company, despite his background as a programmer.

What about Richard Branson? He is not the smartest person in the entire Virgin Group. When you organize a crew of your own, you're essentially saying you're not the person with all the answers. You accept that you are not that smart and you need smart people around you. If you want to attract people who know their stuff, you have to believe that you will not be the smartest person in the room.

People who have an ego problem can't do this. They need to be the most intelligent person in the room. When they see someone smarter than them, they try to eliminate that person.

Be okay with the fact that you are going to be surrounded by people much better than you. A team is as strong as its components, and you have to fill those seats with amazing people who know their stuff inside out. It will give you a competitive advantage over other similar companies.

Be okay with the fact that you are going to be surrounded by people much better than you.

There's another side to that as well. Your team may suggest solutions you're tempted to ignore because of experience. Sometimes too much experience leads to too much ego. As a result, you disregard unorthodox opinions.

Take, for example, the famous case of Blockbuster against Netflix. By the mid-to-late 2000s, Blockbuster was, in fact, investing in its digital businesses. But the CEO who had come in during that time was the former CEO of 7-Eleven, and he put all his cards in the retail side of the business. So despite having an online division, as well as a streaming service gearing up for launch, their focus was on expanding the retail division of Blockbuster. This CEO had people telling him online was the way forward. But he, in all his wisdom, didn't take it to heart. In fact, Blockbuster's leadership saw online as a threat and an inferior side of the entire business. Everybody knows the rest of that story.

But the most important reason why you must check your ego is that if you don't, you won't attract any experts around you. At Maxy Media, I know I have the right people in technology, media buying, and content creation. I encourage these people to put out their honest opinions, and I listen to them with curiosity and humility. I trust them to do their job. That's why I hired them in the first place. It goes both ways. If I don't respect their expertise, why should they stick around and keep working for me?

If you want a good crew, then you need to be CEO, whether you wear that title or not. Chet Scott, the author of *Becoming Built to Lead*, believes each of us is "The CEO of a cool little company called YOU."[15]

On that topic, here's a quick little story about two CEOs. Which one would you like to be? Which one would you like to follow? Red or Blue?

CEO Red is known to have a reputation as someone who berates the employees mercilessly. When things go badly, Red always blames other people. Red somehow manages to find faults everywhere and complains to no end that Red is the only one who does anything around there. Whenever there are instances of failures, Red threatens to fire the employee responsible for it then forces that employee to exhaust himself to correct the mistake. Whenever something good happens, Red takes all the credit. It is the Red show. Red doesn't let anyone take decision-making power but shovels accountability on others.

Then there's the Blue CEO. Every day Blue starts by motivating the employees. Blue gives them positive compliments and clear feedback on their progress. If failures happen, Blue has a meeting with them to discuss what went wrong, what they can do to fix it, and how to refrain from making that mistake again. Blue gives credit where it's due and rewards people for it as well. When times are tough, Blue rallies the employees by empowering them and supporting them as much as possible. Most of all, Blue applies discipline while showing compassion. Blue never loses sight of the bigger picture.

Which crew would you want to be part of? Red or Blue? The answer is clear.

Other people are an intimate part of our success and failure. They affect our career paths and our futures in many ways. In my life, I've experienced many times when a person lifted me up or shot me down.

In light of Le Studio's fallout, I felt like I was drifting around with no anchor to hold me. I had relied on my business partner to show me the way, and all he did was cast me out into darkness. But it was also a friend who had gotten me a call with EVO Canada, which ignited my meteoric rebirth.

Since then, I have learned how the people around you shape your path, and I have done much to cultivate my circle of influence. I sought out people who were beneficial to my growth. I found myself in elevated conditions, surrounded by people who knew more than me, who had more than me and therefore simply had much more to offer me in terms of advice and support. There is a stark difference between hanging out with billionaires and hanging out with homeless people. In most scenarios, one group of people will help you build a better life, while you might help the other group of people build a better life themselves.

It was often during the events organized by Tony Robbins and Dan Sullivan when I found amazing business ideas, often spurring from conversations with the attendees. I became friends with many of them, exchanging advice and recommendations. Some of the most brilliant investment counsel came from these circles.

Your circle of influence is like your advisory board. These are the people who will help you make the right decisions and guide you to where you want to go.

Your right relationships won't appear out of nowhere. You have to establish the right circle of influence that will help you grow into the person you want to become. If you think you can benefit from coaching as I did, this might open up another realm of opportunities for growth in both your personal and professional life.

The most successful people don't wait around for luck to find them. Rather, they make their luck by pursuing the strategies and techniques they feel will ensure them a respectable amount of success.

Without knowing exactly where you want to go, you can't possibly find the right people to help you along the way.

The most successful people don't wait around for luck to find them.

If you want to become a better chess player, you shouldn't hang out with people who simply play checkers. Instead, you should invest time with other chess players. Furthermore, if you want to be a master chess player, don't hang out with any old chess players. You have to be among the best chess players in the world.

Your circle of influence should look similar to the people you want to become. These people have already succeeded in ways you desire, and they can show you the way to greater knowledge, experience, and connections.

I have sought out many mentors in my lifetime. During that search, I often identified the wrong mentors. These people only posed as mentors, but they didn't have much to offer. This was true about the CEO of the company that had acquired ProNet. He was only concerned with his own personal gain. This was my partner in the failed real estate project.

My life completely changed when I found great mentors. Not only that, but these types of mentors also attract a good caliber of students who often become great allies. I got the idea for the fitness business when I attended a platinum event with Tony Robbins and talked with one of the guys I befriended there.

To conclude, your crew, mastermind and circle of influence will greatly determine how lucky you become.

EXTERNAL CONDITIONS

Supplementation

Our bodies don't receive everything they need through normal food and drink. As a result, I highly recommend supplementation. I've been taking supplements for years. The benefits speak for themselves. I have great energy in the morning, and I can work all day into the late hours. My energy level is ten out of ten all day long. Before I knew anything about proper nutrition and supplementation, my energy levels were literally a five out of ten. When I woke up in the morning, I would drag through the day trying to get my "motor started." After a big carbohydrate-filled lunch, I would experience a big afternoon crash. My energy would drop to a two out of ten.

Supplementation is intentionally part of The Lucky Formula because of the common misconception that we can get all the nutrients we need from food.

On the surface, this makes sense. If you eat whole foods that are fresh and unprocessed, you might think you are receiving a proper supply of vitamins, minerals, antioxidants, and other nutrients.

Unfortunately, this just isn't true. Even with a perfect diet, you suffer from other factors outside of your control.

Even with a perfect diet, you suffer from other factors outside of your control.

Some of these factors are:

- depleted soils
- the storage and transportation of our food
- genetically modified foods
- increased stress and nutritional demands resulting from a toxic environment
- environmental pollution
- jet fuel in our bloodstream

These factors make it impossible for us to get the vitamins and minerals we need solely from the foods we eat. Simply put, the evidence shows we cannot get away from the need for nutritional supplements.

Along with my eating regimen, I also consume various supplements, including Omega-3, vitamin B, vitamin C, vitamin D, vitamin K, zinc, calcium, magnesium, MCT oil, and other nutritional supplements that help me with my energy levels and athletic performance.

I've discovered that great health isn't just what you *do* put in your body; it's also what you *don't* put in your body. As a result, I avoid sugar, bad fats, and salt in my food. These are what I consider poison in the body.

You may think I'm crazy for doing this, but it works for me. I think everyone should find a "hack" that works for them. To blindly adopt a plan or routine set by someone else is a surefire way to fail. No person's body is the same as any other.

Besides the internal conditions and the external conditions, we still need one more component to complete The Lucky Formula. Without the right actions, there's no movement and simply no luck. In the next chapter, we'll unpack how we can know what actions to take.

10

Right Actions

I have been impressed with the urgency of doing.
Knowing is not enough. We must apply.
Being willing is not enough. We must do.
—Leonardo da Vinci

Ignorant people downplay action. They sit around and wait for luck to drop from the sky, banking on the belief that luck and laziness go hand-in-hand. As you saw in the last few chapters, this couldn't be further from the truth. When you leverage the right conditions—both internal and external—you stack the odds in your favor for cashing in on success. Action is needed, and the right actions at that.

I love what Will Rogers said: "Even if you're on the right track, you'll get run over if you just sit there." This means when luck smiles upon you, you have to leverage the opportunity. Oftentimes, you don't have a ton of time to think about it.

In a book called *Luck Factor* by psychologist Professor Richard Wiseman, the author identifies what makes people lucky. Wiseman believes lucky people are those who make the most out of chance encounters, always giving it their best shot. Wiseman shared about a woman who responded to various opportunities that eventually led to her being hired as a professional poet, her dream job. Another woman won many contests and competitions, all because she entered over a hundred of them each week. The first woman decided to show up to the opportunities. The other one just cast their net super wide.

If you have not had much luck in your life, it's not that you are unlucky—it's probably that you're not taking enough action.

If you have not had much luck in your life, it's not that you are unlucky—it's probably that you're not taking enough action.

Through my experiences, to maximize luck you need to take six specific actions. I'll list them below and then unpack them one at a time.

1. Develop Leadership Skills
2. Create a Force Multiplier
3. Find Your Leverage
4. Do What you Want to Do
5. Turn Fear into Courage
6. Follow a Morning Routine

1. Develop Leadership Skills

In the book *Extreme Ownership*, Leif Babin, a former Navy SEAL instructor, and Jocko Willink, a retired Navy SEAL officer, tell a story about the infamous hell week.

According to Willink, "The most fundamental and important truths at the heart of extreme ownership: there are no bad teams, only bad leaders."[16]

Their story resonates with me because it depicts the importance of leadership development. Teams of seven men were required to do a series of boat races. Each team was assigned an old inflatable boat that weighed more than 200 pounds. The most senior-ranking sailor in that group became the team leader.

The race involved the teams carrying their boats over their heads up and down the beach. They'd get in the surf and paddle their boats to a designated spot and then back to shore. They would do this over and over again, getting in and out of the boat, paddling and running until the point of absolute exhaustion.

As the races went on, a clear pattern emerged between the teams. Boat Crew 2 came in first place in nearly every race. This was understandable. Boat Crew 2 had a strong leader, and every team member was highly motivated to push themselves. They helped each other and worked together to win as a team.

This was in contrast to Boat Crew 6, a group that came in last place almost every time. Boat Crew 6 was dysfunctional as a team. Rather than working as one, they blamed each other as they grew increasingly frustrated and angry. All of them, including the leader, put their own pain and discomfort before the team's well-being as a whole.

Watching this unfold, the SEAL instructors tried to figure out what was going on with the two teams. What had caused this big gap between them? Suspecting the cause to be based in leadership, the instructors kept their eyes on the leader of Boat Crew 6. He was an inexperienced officer who had lost his temper in each race. This behavior was unacceptable, particularly for a SEAL.

As a result, they changed up the teams. Before the next race, the instructors announced they would switch the leaders of Boat Crew 2 and Boat Crew 6. Babin noticed the struggling crew leader seemed happy about the swap, while the other one looked frustrated but seemed to take this as a challenge.

You might wonder what happened. Did Boat Crew 6 just start dominating while Boat Crew 2 crashed and burned? Not quite. It's a little more complicated than that.

In the next hour, Boat Crew 6 worked as a team and won nearly every race to the instructors' amazement. Whereas Boat Crew 2, though they did not take first, still performed well, nonetheless.

So what happened? It was expected for Boat Crew 6 to do well. After all, they put a superstar leader there, and they were all SEALs essentially. They were all capable soldiers from the start. The new leadership allowed them to unlock their full potential.

In the case of Boat Crew 2, despite the new bad leader, their solid performance was not due to the leader but because of everyone else who had been affected by the good leader before. The superstar leader had brought everyone else up to a level that could not be pushed down, even by a terrible leader. In other words, each SEAL had grown personally.

Babin and Willink elegantly summarize this example: "The most fundamental and important truths at the heart of extreme ownership: there are no bad teams, only bad leaders. Leadership is the single greatest factor in any team's performance."

This is the importance of good leaders. There are no such things as bad teams. But there are definitely bad leaders. There is a truth in Korean, which says, "The downstream is clean, only if the upstream is." You can flip that around too.

If there's dirt coming down from upstream, everything else is going to be dirty too. That's what bad leaders do.

As with the SEAL story, it's not enough to only be a good leader. You have to be a leader who brings up everyone else with you. When this happens, the group builds resilience against bad leadership. Remember, Boat Crew 6 was the worst team almost every time, and the leader of that team went to Boat Crew 2, whose performance didn't completely tank. Thus, good leadership is like nutrients for an organization. They keep everyone going during the bad times, and they motivate all those around them to keep winning.

I've learned that leading is not only about charging ahead, making decisions, and being charismatic. Leadership is also about empowering people, fostering an environment of mutual respect, and building a strong camaraderie.

Every Thursday morning at Maxy Media, I host a thirty-minute call with my employees, in which I give my weekly leadership mentoring sessions. Each time, I tackle different aspects of leadership, and I ask them to apply the lessons to their tasks as much as they can.

> **Leadership is also about empowering people, fostering an environment of mutual respect, and building a strong camaraderie.**

I also regularly look out for who has the makings of a good leader and provide guidance. I give people chances to step up whenever there is an opportunity, and I'm thrilled when people volunteer to take on a new responsibility. In such cases, I throw my support behind them and try to help them succeed. Simply put, I try to nurture leaders within my organization by actively welcoming them and educating everyone on what leadership is.

People often hesitate to step up, and the extra nudge goes a long way in bringing people out of their shells to realize their potential.

There is a big debate between whether leaders are born or made. Some studies say it's a genetic thing and that their brains are just wired differently for effective leadership. Others say leadership is a result of experiences that shape a person to be that way.

Believing leaders are born implies non-leaders can never become leaders. I strongly disagree with this premise, and I only need to look as far as my own life for an example.

When I started at ProNet, I was no leader. I certainly wasn't ready to lead anyone, let alone a company. I ran a two-person partnership with my girlfriend at the time. At the end of the day, I let a guy take over the whole thing during an acquisition and do whatever the hell he wanted while I just rode his coattails.

Afterward, I did get my chance at honing my leadership skills with Pivotal Payments, but I had no system. I tried to lead purely based on instinct, so I made mistakes all over the place. This was before I had leadership mentors.

Ultimately, I experienced my biggest failure in leadership when I didn't take charge of my investments during a real estate venture. I let a guy hustle me and drain me of all my cash. He led me down the path of oblivion, and I let it all happen.

After this, I finally decided to get out of the real estate business and take charge of my life. This was when I began the journey of becoming a leader.

2. Create a Force Multiplier

A force multiplier is a concept rooted in military science. It's defined as "anything that allows something or someone to achieve a greater effect than without it." A force multiplier can be anything, like a piece of equipment that gives a superior advantage to a unit. One example is night vision goggles. Soldiers with night vision goggles can operate at night and see as clear as day. In contrast, a group without night vision goggles will be only half as effective. In fact, the group with night-vision goggles will likely decimate this unit.

A force multiplier can also be something intangible, such as psychology. Dwight D. Eisenhower, who led the Allies to victory in Europe during World War II, famously said, "Morale is the greatest single factor in successful wars."

In his mind, morale stacked the odds in his favor. Morale is often much more important than the actual force you have. But conversely, if a psychological campaign can lower the morale of an enemy unit, this is an example of a force multiplier in reverse.

Sometimes a force multiplier is a strategy or a tactic that gives you a significant advantage in an otherwise deadlocked situation. One of the most famous examples of this is the German blitzkrieg, applied during World War II.

At that time, war was generally a static affair. Two opposing sides hid in their respective trenches. They pummeled each other with shells, trying to beat the other through sheer numbers of troops and more supplies. But when World War II began, the Germans did something different. They ignored conventional tactics and focused all their firepower, including airplanes, tanks, and mechanized infantry, into a single focal point on the front. This allowed them to push through the frontline quickly and overwhelm the enemy before they could mount a counterattack.

This was super effective for the Germans because not only did it dislocate the defenders from their positions, but they couldn't properly regroup to put on a more effective defense. Every time the defenders tried to rally, the Germans would already be there, obliterating their next target. This was how they could swiftly take large territories by surprise and surround their enemies, which resulted in early surrender.

But it's not only in the military doctrine that force multipliers can be used. They can easily be applied in any context. In sports, an unconventional recruiting method could give a team a significant advantage. This is what happened with the Oakland Athletics in 2002 when Billy Beane turned to statistics to assemble a competitive baseball team with only a small budget available.

Billy Beane applied a concept called sabermetrics, highlighted in a best-selling book called *Moneyball*. This method consisted of measuring the empirical performance of players on the field and making analyses according to those measurements. As a result, the Oakland Athletics had a dynamite 2002 season, with a record-breaking twenty consecutive wins. Sabermetrics was the force multiplier for the Oakland Athletics.

This happens in business too. In fact, it happens all the time. Every once in a while, a company comes around and disrupts the entire ecosystem. It runs circles around existing giant companies, scaling faster and taking market share, beating out the competition. In every case of "David taking out Goliath," there's always a force multiplier.

Take, for instance, Airbnb. How did a company that purportedly has no real estate inventory become a titan in an industry, beating out large established brands? The answer is technology, which allows anyone to open a bed and breakfast. This meant Airbnb could expand with less limitation, whether through geography or capital. They didn't have to buy a house or lease it long term to open a new location in, say, Lisbon.

The same thing goes for ride-sharing companies such as Uber and Lyft. These firms crushed the taxi industry by relying on one significant piece of technology—GPS. There's a reason why driving cabs used to be more of a licensed industry. Of course, this was due to the experience and knowledge one needed in maneuvering the streets without reliance on maps. GPS changed all that, literally allowing anyone to become a cab driver by providing the best route to any destination.

I've used force multipliers to my advantage many times throughout my business career. I've seen what they can do. When you have a force multiplier on your side, everything becomes easier. Your results double, triple, or even multiply by ten. It systematizes luck because it's an engine that maximizes opportunities, and your luck balloons into a culture of success.

A force multiplier works because it allows you to do more with the same resources or even less. This is not only about saving time or cutting costs. These are important. But where a force multiplier truly excels is creating new opportunities.

If you look at many of the technology companies that have exploded on the scene, you'll see this time and time again. It favors scalability. Everyone I know wants their businesses to scale fast and outgrow the competition. When things scale, your lean company of ten suddenly grows to one hundred. Revenues start adding zeros to the end, and that also goes the same for your valuation.

With force multipliers, an input of one can grow to an output of ten or one hundred. If you're looking to achieve success on a large scale, a force multiplier is a must. With it, everything can be easier, faster, and with greater effects than you could have imagined.

You might think a force multiplier has to be grandiose or complex and push the limits. But oftentimes, a force multiplier is a very simple thing. All you have to know is where to apply the force multiplier, and once you have that figured out, everything will start to click.

Here are three simple steps to create your own force multiplier:

(1) Identify your bottlenecks.

A bottleneck is any point of congestion within a system. Not all bottlenecks are equal. Based on my experiences, there are two main types of bottlenecks. One is when an influx of work suddenly causes a temporary blockage. This is most likely a blessing in disguise because it can be dealt with by simply working harder during this time. All this new business can be used as a platform for a bigger leap forward.

The real toxic kind of bottleneck is one that prevents growth. It could be something as simple as a lack of resources. It could also be a matter of not having the right personnel or not having your personnel in the right conditions. An A+ employee will not turn out top-grade work if placed in a C- environment. When a bottleneck prevents growth, it results in negative effects for the company in the long run. One primary problem is that a competitor can more easily overtake you and crush you. Everything could also become harder, from maintaining a healthy balance sheet to attracting top talent.

When EVO Canada started, our main problem was that the only source of sales was me, the company's CEO, and a handful of others. If we wanted to grab market share quickly, we had to expand. There were competitors and copycats hot on our heels, and we could only succeed through quickly assembling a sales team for the company. Once we knew about this bottleneck, we could move forward with solving this problem.

(2) Clearly outline your solution.

Once you figure out the bottleneck, you need to address the problem. This is where you need to assess your situation carefully and concretely determine what you must do.

To do this, you have to gain insight into the limitations you have as well as what others are doing. Depending on the actions of your competitors, the details of this solution may have to change.

For EVO Canada, once I realized I needed to up our sales game, we tried to put together a great sales team. However, we didn't have a huge budget to hire a massive sales division. We would have needed millions of dollars to launch a rock-star sales team right out of the gates, and that wasn't going to happen immediately.

On top of this, we had a limited window of time to gain market share. As I mentioned, Pivotal's Cardex was also in the market and competing with us in the Canadian sector. This was a big existential threat to us. Pivotal was right there in Montreal, positioned and funded to use Cardex to blitz through Canada.

Not only did we have to hire new people without a budget, but we had to do it quickly. This may sound like an obvious solution, but clearly outlining it enabled us to think about finding a solution. This leads us to the next critical step.

(3) Create a mechanism that makes the solution work.

Oftentimes, just identifying a solution is not enough. You need to also come up with real mechanisms that work for your specific set of contexts.

We knew a non-salaried sales position would get scoffed at because most people value salaried jobs. The Great Recession had just happened,

Oftentimes just identifying a solution is not enough.

and people were looking for security more than anything. We also knew people would have trouble generating leads from scratch when they first joined us. We were hardly in a position where we could ask for a superstar sales team to work for us because we did not have the cash to do that.

To overcome this bottleneck, we came up with our own non-salaried sales model. Implementing the model was not enough. We needed to give our non-salaried sales team an extra edge—Our version of the "The Ultimate Sales Machine."

At EVO Canada, we came up with a two-fold strategy. First, we created a recruitment process tailored to communicate our massive advantage and establish rapport with the candidates even before they began working. We started by vetting resumes through online posts and print classifieds.

After that, we invited people to our webinars so we could explain the sales method, process, and more importantly, how much they could make in dollar terms. In these webinars, I tried as much as possible to paint a picture of where they could be and what they could become if they followed our sales formula.

This was super effective. Once people were in the webinars, 80 percent of them were convinced. We gained several associates with each webinar we hosted. This allowed us to swiftly build up a large sales organization of more than a hundred sales executives. It gave us a huge chunk of the market share in Canada.

Second, we created a process that would elevate the effectiveness of each salesperson. We knew the commission-based compensation approach would be more attractive if people knew they could generate a more reliable income. This is why we introduced a warm lead system. We generated all the leads from our telemarketing team. We booked the appointments and then passed them onto the sales executives in the field.

This cushioned the risk for our non-salaried sales team, and it also increased the success rate of each sales executive while significantly decreasing the most tedious part of sales, which was knocking on doors and generating leads in the first place.

We had created two force multipliers: a recruitment webinar and the warm lead sales system. This made our sales process more cost-efficient and scalable.

You may wonder, what is your own force multiplier? Before you begin designing yours, remember the need for you to have an experimental mind. Even the great blitzkrieg was a fruition of a long evolution of military tactics that started with the storm troopers in WWI. This tactic, while similar in fashion, was much more elementary and also mildly successful at best.

A force multiplier is strictly an empirical concept. A solution may be theoretical, but the mechanism for your solution has to work in the real world. You may end up trying multiple times to find something that sticks. If something doesn't work at first, try again and again, and eventually, you will find your own force multiplier that works for you.

3. Find Your Leverage

The physics of a lever is fascinating. A lever is a beam or a rod positioned above a hinge that goes up and down like a seesaw. This lever can balance two objects on either side and, depending on the object's distance to the hinge, enable a very small object can be used to lift a much heavier and bigger object. Essentially, it allows someone or something the ability to exert a force much bigger than themselves.

When an opportunity comes knocking, you may find yourself in a situation in which you cannot take advantage of it. Maybe you don't have the proper resources, such as money or people. Perhaps you can't draw funds from a bank because your credit is too low.

But what if there were a way to use something relatively small to produce a big outcome? This is possible with leverage.

When life turns against you, luck creates leverage if you're willing to take action. This is exactly what I did in the worst moment of my business career—the Le Studio deal. I had poured my precious millions into it, and I got backed into a corner, flat broke. But at that moment, when all seemed to be lost, I found my leverage, and my luck changed.

Assess what you have.

The first step to finding leverage is to know exactly what you have. I'm not talking exclusively about your assets, such as how much cash you have or how much equity you've got. These things are very effective levers, but many times we find ourselves lacking tangible assets. To be fair, if you are someone in desperate need of leverage, you probably aren't flush with capital. Most likely, you have debts to pay and bills to take care of, with not much liquidity on hand.

Leverage is so much more than that. I discovered two types of leverage during my dark days of the Great Recession: experience and reputation.

The Leverage of Experience

The experience you have accumulated is the first obvious lever you have at your disposal. When I called my friends asking for help, I got an introduction to the founder of EVO Payments International. Immediately, they were looking for someone to take them to the Canadian market.

I pounced on the opportunity and pitched that I would lead the Canadian division of EVO. Going into this meeting, I wanted to emphasize two things. I already had extensive experience building a payment company from scratch into millions in recurring revenue. I was also an expert when it came to the landscape of payment processing in Canada. Because I had the right experience for what they wanted to accomplish, I was their perfect man.

In the end, I got a great deal. I was given 30 percent of the Canadian division of EVO payments and would be put in charge of it all.

That deal was 100 percent a result of me leveraging my experience to the maximum. I showcased my assets, and they put their trust in me.

How can you leverage your experience? Discover what the other party needs, and then showcase your assets to meet those needs.

Discover what the other party needs, and then showcase your assets to meet those needs.

The Leverage of Reputation

The story doesn't end here. Remember, I needed to invest $200,000 of my own money into this venture in exchange for 30 percent of the company. That was all great, except I did not have this money. I barely had the airfare to fly to New York to execute this deal and return. I needed to figure out a way to get the money somehow.

How do you generate cash when you have none, and the banks won't lend you any because you don't qualify for any of the options they offer?

I decided to fundraise. Once they promised me 30 percent of the shares of this new payments' company in Canada, I went out on a fundraising run to raise money for 5 percent of those shares.

I received a ton of NOs, but I only needed one YES. I leveraged my reputation to do this.

Your reputation is important leverage. People's desire to associate with you has value, and that value becomes bigger if you have a good reputation. Make sure to keep good track of your reputation. It works wonders if you are in a pinch.

> **People's desire to associate with you has value, and that value becomes bigger if you have a good reputation.**

Fortunately, I had an excellent reputation in the Canadian payments processing industry, as well as the greater business community. I leveraged that to my advantage. Needless to say, I raised the money.

Combine your leverages.

There's something called the compound lever, a machine that operates on using the resistance from one lever as the effort for the next lever. Simply put, it's a lever on a lever. It increases the mechanical advantage of the machine, particularly when there is a restriction of space.

Let's say you need to lift a heavy load that requires a plank fifty feet long. If you only have space for twenty-five feet of plank, you can divide the plank into two and stack the levers on top of each other. When you put the weight on the first lever, the resistance from the first lever presses down on the second lever with twice as much force, allowing you to achieve what you wanted to do in the first place.

This is the perfect metaphor for what I did at EVO Canada.

Once the deal went through with EVO Payments, I knew I would get the shares if I had the money. But I had very little wiggle room. I couldn't borrow the money from the bank, and I certainly didn't have the money myself.

As long as the certainty of the money was close to 100 percent, I could use the shares as leverage to raise capital, then use that capital to pay off what I needed to get EVO Canada launched.

I combined two levers. One was the original lever, which was how I negotiated with EVO Payments with my experience. But that lever was not strong enough to lift the whole thing off the ground. Then I stacked the lever of the equity on top of it, which finally allowed me to pull through. I raised $300,000, more than I had to pay initially.

I encourage you to combine levers. Find where they overlap. Once you identify the focal point, combine your leverages and figure out how to ensure you can do more with less.

With only one lever, I would not have been able to raise the necessary capital, which would have meant no EVO Canada either. However, by using a compound lever, I generated $300,000 in addition to obtaining 30 percent of a new company that had the backing of a major corporation.

I did all of this while having zero dollars to my name. An outsider might chalk it up as luck. I redefine it as leverage.

Figure out what the other wants.

Everything has value. The products you buy, the food you eat, and the media you consume—they all have value. This is market value, driven mainly by supply and demand, which we all commonly refer to as price. Price is applied uniformly to everyone. Whether you are a banker or a cab driver, a Big Mac costs exactly the same price.

Then there is something called economic value. This is a value measured by how much one has to gain from the good or service. It's more relative than market value.

For example, let's say I have a toy, a limited collector's version I got as a gift from a friend. It cost fifty dollars. If I am not a fan of the toy, I have no added value attached to it.

Imagine one day someone sees it and immediately wants to buy it for $150. I'm shocked because I thought it was $50. This collector sees a premium of $100 on top of that. Little did I know, he is a huge collector of these toys, and this particular toy is the one missing from his grand collection. In fact, in this guy's mind, the price is much higher than $150. This is the *economic* value.

Leverage is a two-way street. There's always someone at the other end of the lever you are trying to pull down. Just as you want something out of the leverage you have, the other person wants something as well. You have to always assume the other is also trying to pull the lever as much as you are. Everyone has their own interests, and you have to find out the other's interests to use your leverage effectively.

When I finally grew tired of my time at EVO Canada, I decided to exit. My lawyer hinted that EVO Payments, the parent company, would go public and buy out its minority shareholders.

This was not public information at the time, but we made a judgment call. We saw the signs and decided we would hold out to get the most out of this deal. Relatively speaking, time was on our side. The more the initial public offering was delayed, the more desperate EVO's leadership would be to get my shares free from my hands. My shares were essentially more valuable to them than they were to me. I used that knowledge as leverage to get a better price.

If you can correctly deduce what the other person wants, you can use that knowledge to push your advantage further. Of course, you must be very careful doing this because you are trying to figure out someone else's intentions. Only act on this kind of leverage when you have done proper research.

> **If you can correctly deduce what the other person wants, you can use that knowledge to push your advantage further.**

They say fortune favors the bold. You have to be bold in your leverage if you hope to seize an opportunity coming your way.

When I walked into that office to pitch to EVO Payments, I mustered every last bit of courage I had to pull it off. If I had walked in there being my depressed self from a few weeks before, I would not have been seen as anyone to do business with. Also, if I had pitched that same depressed way to my potential investors without showing the confidence of having 30 percent of a company, they would have never given me any money.

Don't be timid when using leverage. You might think, "Aren't I faking it?'" But you aren't. You have leverage. That is an asset in itself. Be brave, and lady luck will smile upon you.

4. Do What You Want to Do.

All the money in the world won't make you happy if you hate what you're doing. Jon Bon Jovi said it another way: "Nothing is as important as passion. No matter what you want to do with your life, be passionate."

I wasn't always passionate; case in point: when I first got lucky with ProNet, the first payments' company that I ran. It was acquired by a company and subsequently put on the stock market. Instantly, I became a paper millionaire.

All the money in the world won't make you happy if you hate what you're doing.

I couldn't really use this luck to my advantage. Long story short, because of details in the contract during the acquisition of my company, I couldn't unload my shares when the time was right. Subsequently, the dot-com bubble burst before I could make my fantastic exit, and all I got left with was a major tax bill.

I would have more chances to cash in on lady luck and make a windfall from owning equity in a company. Time and time again, it happened. With Pivotal, I made off with a hefty amount of cash at the end of my tenure there. With another payments' company, I received my promised shares and cashed in on them later when the company went public. And I exited EVO Canada at just the right time, leveraging all my knowledge to get the most out of my shares. Being lucky takes practice. If luck comes to you, but you have no clue how to use it to your advantage, you might as well not have had it at all. So how do you practice luck?

Great question! The answer is simply by doing what you *want* to do.

I like building companies. It's what gets me going. I like to strategize and execute on plans. That's what I want to do when I go to work on a given day. I don't want to occupy myself with minute details or minor operational problems. By fiercely sticking with what I want to do, I gained equity in a valuable company several times. The first time, I completely blew it. But for the rest of them, because I leveraged my experience, I engaged in a profitable exit.

The only time I failed in spectacular fashion was when I took myself out of my element. This was the case with the real estate guru. I have never made this mistake again. Now, I do what I want to do, and I don't let anything distract me.

The hustle culture tells people they should always be working. Many people follow this advice and exhaust themselves doing literally everything. I was that person. There was a time I tried to insert myself into every single decision-making process and discussion in the company because I thought, *I'm the CEO, so I should know everything and do all of it myself.*

That isn't true at all, in practice or theory. First of all, this is an unsustainable way to work and a major contributor to burnout. You are one person, and there is a limit to what you can do. That email box full of tasks used to haunt me. I dreaded it, and just opening it gave me anxiety.

At some point, this anxiety, coupled with the monotony I felt at EVO, made me realize I didn't need to run every aspect

> **You are one person, and there is a limit to what you can do.**

of the business. As long as I hired the right people in the right places, I could leave those parts to the experts and focus on what I enjoyed doing.

You have a purpose in what you want to do.

There's a psychological concept called flow, coined by psychologist Mihaly Csikszentmihalyi. Flow is a state of heightened focus in which you are optimized for productivity. In flow, you are totally immersed in the activity. Think of an ice hockey player who is on top of his game. The puck seems to stick to him. He weaves in and out of other players as if they were standing still. He passes and receives the puck with ease, wherever he is. He can spot an opportunity at any given moment and takes the perfect shot to put the puck in the net. He's in tune with his movements and in complete control. This is a flow state.

The most critical element, according to Dr. Csikszentmihalyi, is to clearly know your goals. This is true for both micro-objectives with activities you do, as well as your larger, overarching purpose. If we take the hockey player example, the goal of a pass is getting the puck to another teammate. A shot on the opposing team's net has the goal of scoring. And the overarching goal of all these actions combined is to win the game and ultimately the championship at the end of the season.

As soon as EVO was established and running like a smooth engine, we had the goal to be the number one payments' company in Canada. To do that, we needed a massive investment, but my partners simply didn't want to commit big dollars to the Canadian market. And this was coupled with the fact that I realized it was time to sell the company. My passion was in building something big, but others did not share that vision. As a result, I found myself disengaging, losing my sense of direction.

When I left EVO, I tapped into this passion for building big things. I flipped a switch internally. When I was building the fitness center from one to more than two dozen locations and growing Maxy Media to one of the top TikTok advertisers in North America, I felt compelled by a purpose. Every move I made flowed.

You have razor-sharp focus.

When you love what you do, focus comes easier. You concentrate harder and become exponentially more productive. No one needs to motivate you. I'll use my son as an example. Early on, when he started school, he had difficulty focusing on the material. I would constantly get feedback from teachers that he was disruptive and choosing to distract other kids. It got so bad that the teachers recommended we put him on medication to calm him down at one point. I was totally against that.

When you love what you do, focus comes easier.

I had observed him when he was playing with a Lego set; he was absolutely zeroed in. For hours he'd sit and build something amazing. The same went for when he was in judo. He has a natural love for the sport. It's true that he's usually distracted easily, but during judo, his mind was completely engaged. That focus has translated into his rapid improvement at judo. His improvement in the sport has impressed everyone, including his coach.

I've also had similar experiences. When I was building the fitness centers, I loved every moment of it. It was why I could focus all my attention on it, leading to an exponential expansion of the fitness locations.

The case is clear. You need to love what you do because it makes you focus. And when you focus, that's when the magic happens. No one gets lucky without focus.

Figure out what makes you tinker.

Most people don't know what they really like doing. They sort of drift through their careers, not paying attention to the signs of what makes them tick.

However, you owe it to yourself to figure that out, regardless of your age. You're never too young or too old.

Follow your bliss. If you enjoy something just for the sake of it, that's a big clue.

Think carefully about what activities you truly enjoy and what you don't. Reflect on what feelings you had when you were doing certain things. This is when introspection is needed.

When I think back to the moments I felt complete joy, they were always when I was growing a business from the ground up. And the best moments were when I strategized for explosive growth.

I felt bored or distracted when I got bogged down by operational monotony and repetitive tasks. It's not that these things are not important. I'm just not great at managing the constant day-to-day tasks because it always drains me. Some people are great at it, but it's not for me.

I figured out what makes my heart beat faster by examining my past. This may sound like a simple exercise, but it requires honesty. Don't think about what you are good at or what other people say you should do. Follow your bliss. If you enjoy something just for the sake of it, that's a big clue.

Prioritize tasks and eliminate tasks.

The best way to pursue only what you want to do is to prioritize tasks and eliminate tasks. In the myriad of things you must do every day, there has to be at least a few things you would be better off without.

I don't want to be concerned with everyday operations. I only want to know things are running smoothly so I can focus on what matters for me, which is growing the business.

If you don't have someone to delegate your least favorite tasks to, try to figure out how to minimize them. Is there an automation tool you can use to avoid wasteful manual labor?

Or better yet, try to find a way to do without it. If you're terrible at social media and you don't want to do social media marketing, is there another way you can get your business out there? Or is there somebody who can do this for you?

Stick to what you like. This does not mean you should throw out everything else. Find a way to keep track of things and stay informed, rather than being directly involved.

You will come across many opportunities in your life, and one of them is bound to be your lucky break. But for that to happen, you need to stick with doing the things that make you happy.

I only got lucky in the payments' business because I kept going at it. Determined to build a massive payments' company, I focused on my passion for growing things. So it was only a matter of time before I got lucky at some point.

Could the same thing have happened to me if I had stuck with being a sports agent? I think so. Even after losing my core clientele, if I was truly passionate about searching for the best players, I could have become someone legendary, like Don Meehan, who built Newport Sports Management. But I didn't. Rather, I fell into the job and the supposed glamour of it. When that lost its shine, and especially when I became disillusioned with the industry as a whole, my desire to go on completely evaporated. My heart wasn't aligned with the job, and it was best to move on.

Now I stick to what I want to do, and I cut out anything that doesn't align with that goal. So far, it has worked out incredibly.

5. Turn Fear Into Courage.

If we wait to take action until we are fearless, we'll be waiting a very long time. Fear is not your enemy—inaction is. Courage requires fear. If there is no fear, then there is no need for courage. Mark Twain says it this way, "Courage is resistance to fear, mastery of fear, not absence of fear."[17]

The following story illustrates this truth. During the late 1500s, the Japanese invaded the Koreans, starting the Imjin War. The Japanese were very well prepared, and they also had superior firepower, having massively imported European guns and ammunition. The Korean army was getting obliterated. Its navy was crushed, led by an incompetent admiral. The king was on the run, and the fate of the country seemed to be sealed.

With only thirteen ships remaining from the last disastrous battle, Admiral Yi Sun-sin was hastily appointed by the government to defend the country. He rallied what was left of the navy to face the Japanese at a place called Myeongnyang.

This was seemingly an impossible fight. The incoming Japanese fleet had more than 300 ships, while the Koreans only had thirteen.

Understandably, fear was rampant across Yi's side. Most soldiers, even the officers, considered deserting the battle. Yi knew of the fear that gripped his men, and he knew they would surely lose with their morale so low.

He focused on imparting courage to these scared men. Before this battle, he famously said to his generals, "Those who seek death shall live; those who seek life shall die."[18]

The quote is now one of the most renowned sayings in Korea, and it is a reflection of how significant a change of perspective is. Yi told his generals that despite their fears for their lives, having the courage to face the enemy was the best chance for their survival. In essence, they needed to turn their fear into courage.

The following day, facing a much larger force, the Koreans achieved a stunning victory, destroying thirty enemy ships while losing none. The Japanese side lost so many soldiers that half of their officers were left dead or wounded.

They had succeeded in this battle by turning their fear into courage. This was the turning point of the war, which allowed the Koreans to be victorious over the Japanese in the end.

These days, real life rarely gets as desperate as the situation above. The typical person won't find themselves on the eve of a battle that will decide the fate of their nation. But it proves a point. In the darkest hour, you can turn your fear into courage and win.

In the darkest hour, you can turn your fear into courage and win.

It is far too easy to be caught in the death spiral of fear. The majority of people run when darkness falls, and they miss out on luck in the process. The simple fact is that luck and fortune do not happen to the fearful. Those filled with fear don't take action. Rather, they remain "frozen" in fear, and luck passes them by.

Only the courageous seize the day and take advantage of opportunities that come to them. As Virgil wrote in the *Aeneid*, "Fortune favors the bold."[19]

I've experienced fear many times in my life, and it felt like drowning in quicksand. Everything is breaking apart around you, and you are scared to death about the next bad thing that will happen. You feel hopeless and helpless. You need to reach deep inside and find Admiral Yi's courage and this can be done by embracing every aspect of The Lucky Formula.

Embrace reality.

In his book *Principles*, Ray Dalio talks about how to become a hyperrealist and embrace the world for what it is. He says you should not get hung up on how you perceive the world should be and instead take it as it is.[20] He's right.

Fear comes from the discrepancy between how we think the world should be and how it actually is. The world can be unforgiving and brutal. When you set out to achieve something great and get knocked down, you may think to yourself, "This is not how it should be." That mindset doesn't serve you. Rather, you need an upgrade.

This is possible when you embrace reality. Take the world as it is, not as how you think it should be. Once you do, you realize that fear is simply an irrational reaction, one that doesn't serve you.

When I got knocked down because of the Le Studio debacle, I dove into a deep depression. At some point, I decided just to wake up because I knew nothing was going to change as long as I sat on my butt and moped. The reality was that I had lost money, and nothing I did would change that fact. I refused to die, and I took productive action instead. I picked up the phone and started dialing to create opportunities. I decided to make my luck, and the rest is history.

That is the beauty of reality. Sometimes reality is against you, and you can't do anything about it. But then there are times when reality gives you a tailwind. It can flip from one side to the other just like that. If you embrace reality for what it is, you will eventually learn to walk on the side that makes you more successful.

If you embrace reality for what it is, you will eventually learn to walk more on the side that makes you more successful.

Remember your best times.

One strategy that helped me dig myself out of my personal hell was realizing the best version of myself still lived within me. I wasn't Mark Lachance, a failed real estate investor. I was Mark Lachance, a successful serial entrepreneur in the payments industry.

I reminded myself I once negotiated contracts for some of the best athletes in the world, putting together deals for multimillion-dollar salaries with owners of National Hockey League teams. At a payments' company, I negotiated my way out and still retained my shares. Time and time again, I stood up to people far wealthier than me who had far more influence.

All of this was still within me. I didn't suddenly become someone else. I was still all those best versions of myself. That truth helped me take action and face my fear. I found the courage to get out there again. I tapped into who I still was and negotiated that killer deal with EVO Payments. From that point on, everything in my life rose like a rocket ship.

In your lowest moments, think of the times when you've shined. Don't let your failures and your fear cloud your judgment of who you are. The person you once were is still there. Become that person again and dare to go further.

Shift from a problem-focused mindset to a solution-focused mindset.

Weird question, but do you know what a Weeble is? It's basically a round-bottomed doll that is hollow inside. The doll has a weight placed in the lower half so that when you push it over, the doll wobbles a bit, but it pops right back up. No matter how many times you push this toy over, it pops into an upright position.

When you focus on the problems, you focus on what's going wrong. This is why you have to switch to a solution-focused mindset and become a Weeble. Remember their slogan? "Weebles wobble, but they don't fall down."

Every time you think, *I have this problem, and I don't know what to do about it*, switch your perspective. Instead, say, "What can I do about this problem?"

Is there a solution you can apply to the problem that will make the situation better? Is there a secondary problem connected to that problem? Come up with a solution for that second problem. Stay in a creative mindset, not a critical one.

At the height of my depression, I focused on the bills and losing money. But this was the wrong approach. What I should've done was ask myself how I could get the money coming in again.

This shift in perspective enabled me to generate money out of nowhere after the EVO Canada deal. I had to invest $200,000 for 30 percent of the company, according to the deal. If I had still been in my problem-focused mindset, I would have crumbled and given up. Instead, I weaved my way out. I figured out a solution and raised money by selling a portion of the shares they had promised me.

Fear expands when you sit still and focus on your problems. But courage shows up when you take action and figure out a solution.

> **Fear expands when you sit still and focus on your problems. But courage shows up when you take action and figure out a solution.**

Admiral Yi faced an impossible battle, but he had confidence he'd win. He had carefully coordinated to draw the Japanese into a narrow strait, where they could not fan out to surround the Korean navy. There was only one passage to get to the Koreans, and the Koreans only had to pummel the enemy with their long-range cannons. Only when Admiral Yi managed to snap them out of their fear could they win the battle. Those who turn fear into courage leverage luck. They open their eyes and spot the opportunities in front of them.

In *Julius Caesar*, William Shakespeare wrote, "Cowards die many times before their deaths; The valiant never taste of death but once."[21] Our minds can imagine so many ways we might die. Most of them never happen. Do not suffer all the deaths that fear makes you go through. Tap into courage. Turn your darkest moment into your finest triumph.

❦ ❦ ❦

Can you be lucky without taking a risk?

That is a great question. I believe luck visits us, but unless we take a risk and act, we'll never cash in on success.

Risk means exposure to threats or danger. Risk means the potential of a loss. Maybe there's a new market a company wants to venture into, but the company is unsure it will make it because there's a huge player already there. Such was the case with Microsoft when it launched Xbox back in 2001.

We all know how Xbox is now one of the three console giants along with Nintendo and Sony, but this could have gone badly for Microsoft. Back then, the Japanese gaming consoles—led by Sony's Playstation 2, Sega's Dreamcast, and Nintendo's GameCube—dominated the market. And this was after the Atari Jaguar, the only American console in the market, folded in the mid-nineties after a humiliating defeat by the Japanese.

The Jaguar only sold a quarter of a million units, dwarfed by even the worst-performing Japanese console, Sega Dreamcast. Going into this venture was a huge risk for Microsoft because not only did it have no experience in the game console market but they were also trying to take market share away from established industry heavyweights. Microsoft came out of the console war as a victor, surviving through the toughest years to become one of the biggest players in the market. Microsoft's gamble turned into a huge success.

Sometimes risk is about choosing between large future gains or small immediate financial rewards. For example, Google's co-founders, Larry Page and Sergey Brin, could have sold the company in 1997 for a relatively small sum of $1.5 million. Nobody knew how Google's future would pan out. Larry Page and Sergey Brin could have pocketed some easy cash to buy a house and move onto the next venture. Instead, they took a risk and leveraged luck. Today Google is valued at several hundred billion dollars.

A culture of risk is therefore critical for growth. You need to set up an atmosphere where breakthrough ideas are welcomed and nurtured, not cast aside as crazy suggestions.

> **Sometimes risk is about choosing between large future gains or small immediate financial rewards.**

In my life, I've experienced many instances of risk. There were times when risk paid off, and there were times when risk let me down. Without risk, I would have probably stuck with my father, working the construction site to this day. I would have collected some money—over a million or so—just enough for retirement.

Despite the ups and downs I've experienced as an entrepreneur, I never regret taking the risk.

Create a culture of risk.

Risk aversion is a natural reaction. Humans don't like to lose. We often fear loss. But fortune doesn't favor those who are afraid. We must be willing to lose for the potential of great reward. Crouching down and hiding get us nothing. Standing tall in the face of great odds opens the door to luck.

Ray Dalio said we should be "radically open-minded." This mindset elevates our perspective and allows us to embrace new ideas. I don't think anyone other than Jeff Bezos ever imagined Amazon would become as big as it is. It was just an online bookstore, after all.

Ideas are definitely a dime a dozen, but only because most of them go untried. So when something new comes your way, be radically open. Don't ever dismiss anything as ridiculous or impossible. Rather, answer these three questions:

1. **Why this idea?** If I told you right now you should invest in something as exotic as wine for dogs, you might laugh. But what if the data proved it? What if pet owners wanted to give their dogs something to drink other than just water? What if a large number of pet owners wanted to "hang out" with their dogs like they would with their best friends? The more data you discover, the less risk the idea requires.

2. **How is it going to benefit you?** Obviously, you can't work on every idea. You have to pick and choose what will contribute meaningfully to what you are doing—particularly if it involves risk. If the idea presented to you doesn't fire you up, then move on. Time is precious.

3. **How can you experiment with the idea?** Risk does not mean you should suddenly move all your chips into one bet. It means trying things out in a controlled manner. If there is a new idea that you like, don't jump on it right away. Instead, try to find how you can experiment with it and build a case for further investment. If your experiment yields good results, then you know you have something with great potential in your hands.

Be coachable.

Right now, I'm the CEO of a digital marketing company. From my past experiences, I understand sales and marketing, but I don't fully understand digital marketing. I'm in an industry I don't exactly know inside and out. So I try to be as coachable as possible. We have resident experts, such as our creative leaders and other employees we've hired, and I listen to them all.

Being coachable means dropping your ego and considering all points of view. You have to be open to the fact that you might not know everything. At Maxy Media, I rely heavily on the expertise of our young creators and media buyers. I have no clue how to present myself in front of a smartphone to make a TikTok video, but our creators can work it like magic.

Being coachable means dropping your ego and considering all points of view.

I've been in many different industries now, including sports, payments, fitness, and marketing. Each time I switched, it was a risk. But I made it because whenever I took that risk, I always sought out smart people to learn from.

Risk often involves not having all the information you need. Most of the time, you will be going into something you aren't familiar with. If you are not coachable when taking a risk, chances are you will flame out very early. Risk punishes those who refuse to learn.

Have the courage to not know.

Risk requires courage. It means you are brave enough to go forth without having a complete picture. There will always be gaps in intelligence, and you often have to make a judgment call.

In *The Attacker's Advantage*, a book by Ram Charan, he talks about "going on the offense" and how it's tied to your tolerance for risk.[22] Making an offensive move in business means moving without all the information you need to feel certain of success. This requires accepting the unknown.

When someone brings you a new idea, there will always be things you can't account for. But you cannot wait for everything to make sense before making a move. Sometimes you have to take a leap of faith.

Big breakthroughs only happen in a culture of risk because it's the great driver of growth. When you create an environment in which people can suggest new ideas freely and also be recognized and rewarded for it, more great ideas will flourish in your organization.

Big breakthroughs only happen in a culture of risk because it's always the great driver of growth.

If you cultivate a culture of risk, people will approach you when they have an idea they want to try out. If you refer to bold ideas as stupid and devalue innovation, no one will ever bring their lucky ideas forward. In that scenario, you drive luck away.

Follow a morning routine

The way you begin your day is a critical factor to jumpstart The Lucky Formula. Your morning routine sets you up to attract or repel luck. For this reason, I've invested significant thought and effort into creating my ideal morning routine. Although we're all different, and so is our ideal morning routine, perhaps seeing mine will inspire you as you create your own.

Each and every day when I wake up, this is what I do:

I open my eyes big and wide and jump right out of bed. I create a positive vibe by repeating these nine affirmations for at least five minutes:

1. I am a fearless leader.
2. I am amazing.
3. I am healthy.
4. I am abundant.
5. I am happy.
6. Life is AWESOME.
7. I am wealthy.
8. I am LUCKY.

And again, thank you, Jake Ducey:

9. The miracle-working universe comes to me and through me, guiding me in EVERYTHING that I do. EVERYTHING that I do SUCCEEDS and PROSPERS beyond my WILDEST imagination.

After the affirmations, I smile in the mirror with a crazy big grin on my face while thinking of something positive and something I am grateful for.

Then I scrape my tongue and clean off the residue that accumulated from the night before. By the way, this is true for all humans. I learned this practice from an Ayurvedic practitioner. Then I brush my teeth with natural mint toothpaste.

Next, I stand in front of a Joovv red light. This is an amazing way to start the day, as the red light gives my cells energy, helps with pain reduction, reduces inflammation from overtraining, and prevents seasonal disorders that I used to get every fall. (I no longer suffer from these symptoms.) I stand in front of the light for ten minutes and then stand with my back to the light for another ten minutes.

After the Joovv light, I jump into the shower. This is where I visualize. (Refer to this previous section for more insight.) I visualize my biggest goal during this particular time in my life.

Once I'm dry, I do ten to fifteen minutes of yoga followed by twenty-one minutes of the inner engineering meditation technique. All of this takes about an hour and ten minutes.

When people first hear this, most say they can't afford to spend that much time doing a morning routine. I understand the pushback. However, the truth is most people can't afford the time *not* to do a morning routine.

Invest in creating the right morning routine. Doing so will determine how lucky you get that day!

The More Risk, the More Awareness, the More Luck

A wonderful byproduct of greater risk is greater awareness. What used to "scare" you five years ago won't "scare" you today. By responding to risk, you grow into a bigger person.

This new awareness sets you up to experience greater levels of luck, evidenced in The Law of Luck©.

The Law of Luck dictates that, by cultivating the right internal and external conditions combined with the right actions, you can stack the odds in your favor and cash in on success.

The Law of Luck dictates that, by cultivating the right internal and external conditions combined with the right actions, you can stack the odds in your favor and cash in on success.

PART 3

Your Future

11

Onto a Fantastic Future

Sooner or later,
those who win are those who think they can.
—Paul Tournier

Congratulations. You've made it to the final chapter. A quick recap will drive the learning deeper.

In Part 1, I shared my flaws, up close and personal. I hope my story was an encouragement to you. After all, if I can get lucky, despite all of the mistakes I've made and failures I've experienced, then you can too.

In Part 2, we took a deep dive into The Lucky Formula. We unpacked the ten internal conditions and the ten external conditions. By adding these right conditions with the right actions, and a combination of risk and awareness, we learned how to stack the odds in our favor to cash in on success.

Right Conditions + Right Actions = Lucky

When I think back to my own life, I realize my opportunities flourished once I changed the conditions inside me and those around me. My team and I grew EVO from zero to hundreds of employees. My wife and I grew the fitness center from one to over twenty locations within a few years. With a superstar team, we catapulted Maxy Media to becoming a top social media advertising agency. These events happened one after the other. Outsiders might say it was a fluke, but I know the truth.

Luck isn't a fluke—it's a formula.

I didn't wait for life to change. Rather, I decided to change. I changed my internal conditions by equipping myself with a better mindset and meditation. Experimenting with biohacks gave me better energy and better health in general.

Luck isn't a fluke—it's a formula.

I changed my external conditions by hanging around people more successful than me, more aligned with my goals. In addition, I invested in mentors who could help guide me in the right direction.

I took action by creating force multipliers that maximized the effects of my inputs. I leveraged my luck by fiercely pursuing what I love doing. I ran toward my fears and cultivated courage. I can honestly say I live a lucky life. The world has opened up to me, and the possibilities from here are endless.

The best news is that The Lucky Formula works for anyone, anytime, anyplace. It's unbiased. If you implement the right conditions with the right actions, you can leverage this formula in your own life.

Don't just learn the formula. Leverage the formula. And when you do, you'll realize your luck is about to change.

Recommended Reading

Achor, Shawn. *The Happiness Advantage: The Seven Principles of Positive Psychology That Fuel Success and Performance at Work.*

Asprey, Dave. *Super Human: The Bulletproof Plan to Age Backward and Maybe Even Live Forever.*

Bach, David. *The Automatic Millionaire: A Powerful One-Step Plan to Live and Finish Rich.*

Canfield, Jack. *The Success Principles: How to Get from Where You Are to Where You Want to Be.*

Clason, George S. *The Richest Man in Babylon.*

Covey, Stephen R. *The 7 Habits of Highly Effective People: Powerful Lessons in Personal Change.*

Dalio, Ray. *Principles: Life and Work.*

Ferriss, Timothy. *Tools of Titans: The Tactics, Routines, and Habits of Billionaires, Icons, and World-Class Performers.*

Frankl, Victor. *Man's Search for Meaning.*

Hill, Napoleon. *Think & Grow Rich.*

Kwik, Jim. *Limitless: Upgrade Your Brain, Learn Anything Faster, and Unlock Your Exceptional Life.*

Pillay, Srinivasan. *The Science Behind the Law of Attraction: A Step-by-Step Guide to Putting the Brain Science Behind the Law of Attraction to Work for You.*

Robbins, Tony. *Awaken the Giant Within: How to Take Immediate Control of Your Mental, Emotional, Physical and Financial Destiny!*

Sullivan, Dan. *Who Not How: The Formula to Achieve Bigger Goals Through Accelerating Teamwork.*

Willink, Jocko and Leif Babin. *Extreme Ownership: How U.S. Navy Seals Lead and Win.*

Notes

Chapter 8: Internal Conditions

1   Sinek, Simon. *Start With Why: How Great Leaders Inspire Everyone to Take Action.* Book description. https://www.amazon.com/Start-Why-Leaders-Inspire-Everyone/dp/1591842808/ref=tmm_hrd_swatch_0?_encoding=UTF8&qid=1630087107&sr=8-3, accessed August 27, 2021.

2   Frankl, Victor. *Man's Search for Meaning.* Boston, MA: Beacon Press, 2006.

3   Hyatt, Gail. "Michael Hyatt & Co Facebook Page." Facebook, May 29, 2020, https://www.facebook.com/michaelhyatt/posts/people-lose-their-way-when-they-lose-their-why-gail-hyatt/10157478188434385/.

4   Kehoe, John. *Mind Power into the 21st Century.* Vancouver, BC: Zoetic, 2011.

5   *Merriam-Webster*, s.v. "self-affirmation (n)," accessed August 26, 2021, https://www.merriam-webster.com/dictionary/self-affirmation.

6   Ducey, Jake. "11 Morning Affirmations for the Most Powerful Morning Routine Ever | Law of Attraction." Uploaded on November 13, 2020. YouTube, 4:50 minutes. https://www.youtube.com/watch?v=eI6K0UyhjOw.

7   Boccia, Maddalena, Laura Piccardi, and Paola Guariglia. "The Meditative Mind: A Comprehensive Meta-Analysis of MRI Studies." BioMed Research International 2015 (2015). https://doi.org/10.1155/2015/419808.

8   Dalio, Ray. Facebook, May 21, 2021, https://www.facebook.com/raydalio/posts/1186816885073318?comment_id=1186956711726002.

9   Robbins, Tony. "Discover Your Peak State: How Emotional Triad Psychology Can Change Your Life." TonyRobbins.com. https://www.tonyrobbins.com/stories/unleash-the-power/discover-your-peak-state.

10   Oberbrunner, Kary. *Unhackable: The Elixir for Creating Flawless Ideas, Leveraging Superhuman Focus, and Achieving Optimal Human Performance*. Ethos Collective. Kindle. 2021.

Chapter 9: External Conditions

11   "Five Reasons Why Women Need More Sleep Than Men." SleepAdvisor. Updated June 9, 2020, https://www.sleepadvisor.org/why-women-need-more-sleep-than-men.

12   "Put the Phone Away! 3 Reasons Why Looking at It Before Bed Is a Bad Habit." Cleveland Health Clinic. April, 22, 2019. Accessed August 27, 2021, https://health.clevelandclinic.org/put-the-phone-away-3-reasons-why-looking-at-it-before-bed-is-a-bad-habit.

13   Robbins, Tony. "How Can I Achieve My Toughest Goals?" TonyRobbins.com. Accessed August 26, 2021, https://www.tonyrobbins.com/ask-tony/how-to-achieve-everything/.

14   Hill, Napoleon. *Think and Grow Rich: The Original Version Restored and Revised*. Anderson, SC: Mindpower Press, 2015.

Notes

15   Scott, Chet. *Becoming Built to Lead: 365 Daily Disciplines to Master the Art of Living*. Ethos Collective, 2020.

Chapter 10: Right Actions

16   Willink, Jocko and Leif Babin. *Extreme Ownership: How U.S. Navy Seals Lead and Win*. New York: St. Martin's Press, 2017.

17   Twain, Mark, and Malcolm Bradbury, ed. *Pudd'nhead Wilson: And Those Extraordinary Twins*. New York: Penguin, 2004. Kindle.

18   Korean Spirit and Culture Promotion Project. "Admiral Yi Sun-Sin: A Brief Overview of His Life and Achievements." Seoul: KSCPP, 2010. Accessed August 31, 2021, https://fromthemixedupfiles.com/wp-content/uploads/2020/12/Admiral-Yi-Sunsin_KSCPP1.pdf

19   Virgil, *The Aeneid*. 29 BC.

20   Dalio, Ray. *Principles: Life and Work*. New York: Simon & Schuster Audio, 2017.

21   Shakespeare, William. *Julius Caesar*, act 2, scene 2, lines 32-33.

22   Charan, Ram. *The Attacker's Advantage: Turning Uncertainty into Breakthrough Opportunities*. Public Affairs, 2015.

About the Author

Mark Lachance is a serial entrepreneur, strategic thinker, and investor. He is a renowned figure in the business world, one who possesses a deep understanding of blitzscaling companies. Having owned and operated several businesses that have experienced hypergrowth through creative business development and lead generation, he is a master of sales and marketing and continues to apply and grow his expertise through current projects.

Mark is the CEO and lead investor of Maxy Media Inc., one of the largest TikTok, Facebook, Snapchat, and Google Display Network performance marketing agencies in the world. Currently, Maxy Media is the number one advertiser in terms of monthly spend on the TikTok platform in Canada and top ten in North America.

In 2016, Mark successfully sold EVO Payments International Canada, an end-to-end payment solutions provider and merchant acquirer which he founded in 2009. He guided the company from its inception with one employee to over 200 employees across Canada.

Prior to founding EVO, Mark was one of the founding members and president of VersaPay Inc, a payments solutions provider, which was taken public in 2010. Before joining VersaPay, Mark was a founding member of Pivotal Payments, which is now a multi-billion-dollar public company. He helped set the foundation and drive the company's sales and revenues before his successful exit from the company in 2006.

Mark has made several other highly successful investments in various industries such as payments, cryptocurrencies, marketing, nutrition, fitness, and sports. Over the past twenty-five years, he has invested in and consulted for dozens of other ventures, which have resulted in highly positive returns.

He speaks and travels the world with his wife, Sonya, and their two boys.

Connect at TheLuckyFormula.com.

How Lucky are You?

Take the Lucky Formula Assessment Today and Get Your Lucky Score©

The Law of Luck says by cultivating the right internal and external conditions combined with the right actions you can stack the odds in your favor and cash in on success.

THE LUCKY FORMULA
ASSESSMENT

Don't be like most people who delay their dreams and goals, hoping and wishing for the perfect time to upgrade their lives. Change your luck, starting now.

TheLuckyFormula.com/assessment

Don't leave luck up to chance.

You've read the book, now it's time to go even deeper with The Lucky Formula Course.

Leverage the Formula in your personal and professional life:

- Powerful case studies from real people generating real results.
- Behind the scenes access into Mark's business playbook.
- Time-tested tactics forged from leadership lessons and best practices.

Start the Course Today.
TheLuckyFormula.com

The Lucky Formula Masterclass

How to Stack the Odds in Your Favor and Cash In on Success

Exclusive access to the advanced concepts, principles, and strategies that Mark Lachance uses on a daily basis to stack the odds in his favor. In this masterclass, you'll receive content typically reserved for private clients. Through raw conversations, lively Q&A sessions, and practical lessons, discover a fast-paced framework to help you leverage The Lucky Formula in your life and business.

- Stop waiting for a lucky break and start stacking the odds in your favor.
- Create an environment of excellence that attracts achievement.
- Cash in on success in a game where you always win.

Enroll at TheLuckyFormula.com/masterclass

The Lucky Formula© Mastermind

Luck is not a fluke. It's a formula.

The Lucky Formula Mastermind is unlike any other experience. It's a way of thinking, being, and doing, designed to grow you and your business exponentially.

- Reclaim the balance you crave: relationally, emotionally, and physically.
- Tap into your hidden ability for superhuman focus to get more done in far less time.
- Organize your life around "flow"—where you feel your best and perform your best.
- Wake up every day thrilled to live your dream.

Culture + Coach + Community + Content

TheLuckyFormula.com/mastermind

Give your audience the luck they crave.

Mark Lachance
author of the bestselling book, *The Lucky Formula*
will show them how to increase success in work and life.

Learn the formula and you'll be inspired.
Leverage the formula and you'll be transformed.
That choice is up to you.

Start the Conversation Today
TheLuckyFormula.com/speaker